THE LEGEND OF KORRA™

Created by
BRYAN KONIETZKO
MICHAEL DANTE DiMARTINO

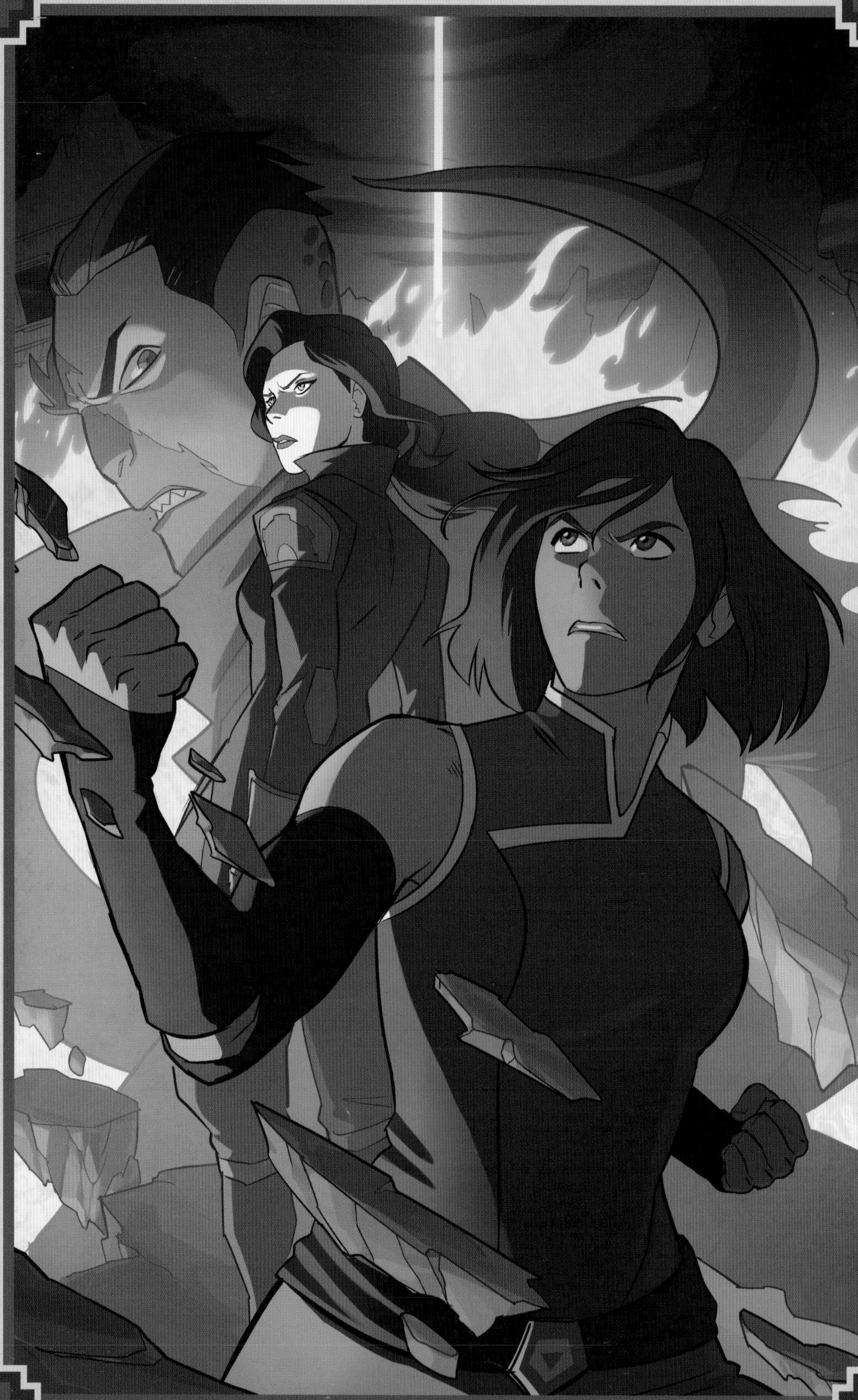

THE LEGEND OF KORRA™

TURF WARS · PART TWO

written by
MICHAEL DANTE DiMARTINO

layouts by
IRENE KOH and **PAUL REINWAND**

art by
IRENE KOH

colors by
VIVIAN NG

lettering by
NATE PIEKOS of Blambot®

cover by
HEATHER CAMPBELL with **VIVIAN NG**

DARK HORSE BOOKS

president and publisher **MIKE RICHARDSON**

editor **DAVE MARSHALL**   assistant editor **RACHEL ROBERTS**

designer **SARAH TERRY**   digital art technician **CHRISTIANNE GOUDREAU**

Special thanks to Linda Lee, Kat van Dam, James Salerno, and Joan Hilty
at Nickelodeon, and to Bryan Konietzko and Michael Dante DiMartino.

Published by **DARK HORSE BOOKS**
A division of Dark Horse Comics, Inc.
10956 SE Main Street, Milwaukie, OR 97222

DARKHORSE.COM | **NICK.COM**

International Licensing: (503) 905-2377
Comic Shop Locator Service: comicshoplocator.com

First edition: January 2018 | ISBN 978-1-50670-040-3

1 3 5 7 9 10 8 6 4 2
Printed in China

Neil Hankerson Executive Vice President • Tom Weddle Chief Financial Officer • Randy Stradley Vice
President of Publishing • Nick McWhorter Chief Business Development Officer • Matt Parkinson Vice
President of Marketing • David Scroggy Vice President of Product Development • Dale LaFountain Vice
President of Information Technology • Cara Niece Vice President of Production and Scheduling • Mark
Bernardi Vice President of Book Trade and Digital Sales • Ken Lizzi General Counsel • Dave Marshall
Editor in Chief • Davey Estrada Editorial Director • Scott Allie Executive Senior Editor • Chris Warner
Senior Books Editor • Cary Grazzini Director of Specialty Projects • Lia Ribacchi Art Director • Vanessa
Todd Director of Print Purchasing • Matt Dryer Director of Digital Art and Prepress • Michael Gombos
Director of International Publishing and Licensing

NICKELODEON THE LEGEND OF KORRA™—TURF WARS PART TWO

Library of Congress Cataloging-in-Publication Data

Names: DiMartino, Michael Dante, author. | Koh, Irene (Comic book artist),
   artist. | Ng, Vivian, colourist. | Piekos, Nate, letterer.
Title: The Legend of Korra : turf wars / written by Michael Dante DiMartino ;
   art by Irene Koh.
Other titles: Legend of Korra (Television program)
Description: First edition. | Milwaukie, OR : Dark Horse Books, 2017- | Part
   one: colors by Vivian Ng ; lettering by Nate Piekos of Blambot ; cover by
   Heather Campbell with Jane Bak.
Identifiers: LCCN 2017015317 | ISBN 9781506700151 (part one : paperback)
Subjects: LCSH: Comic books, strips, etc. | BISAC: COMICS & GRAPHIC NOVELS /
   Media Tie-In.
Classification: LCC PN6728.L434 D56 2017 | DDC 741.5/973--dc23
LC record available at https://lccn.loc.gov/2017015317

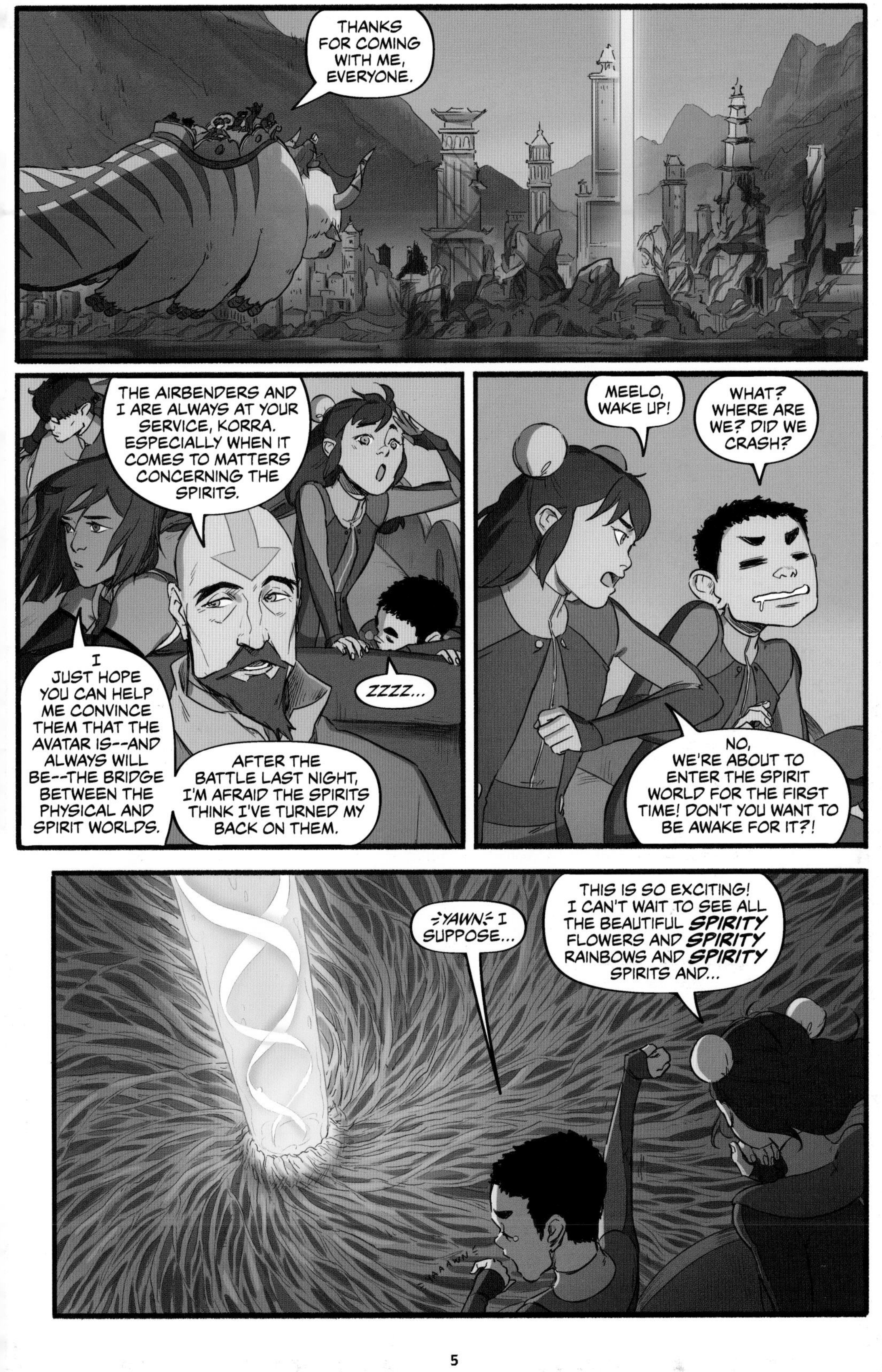
THANKS FOR COMING WITH ME, EVERYONE.
THE AIRBENDERS AND I ARE ALWAYS AT YOUR SERVICE, KORRA. ESPECIALLY WHEN IT COMES TO MATTERS CONCERNING THE SPIRITS.
ZZZZ...
I JUST HOPE YOU CAN HELP ME CONVINCE THEM THAT THE AVATAR IS--AND ALWAYS WILL BE--THE BRIDGE BETWEEN THE PHYSICAL AND SPIRIT WORLDS.
AFTER THE BATTLE LAST NIGHT, I'M AFRAID THE SPIRITS THINK I'VE TURNED MY BACK ON THEM.
MEELO, WAKE UP!
WHAT? WHERE ARE WE? DID WE CRASH?
NO, WE'RE ABOUT TO ENTER THE SPIRIT WORLD FOR THE FIRST TIME! DON'T YOU WANT TO BE AWAKE FOR IT?!
THIS IS SO EXCITING! I CAN'T WAIT TO SEE ALL THE BEAUTIFUL SPIRITY FLOWERS AND SPIRITY RAINBOWS AND SPIRITY SPIRITS AND...
=YAWN= I SUPPOSE...

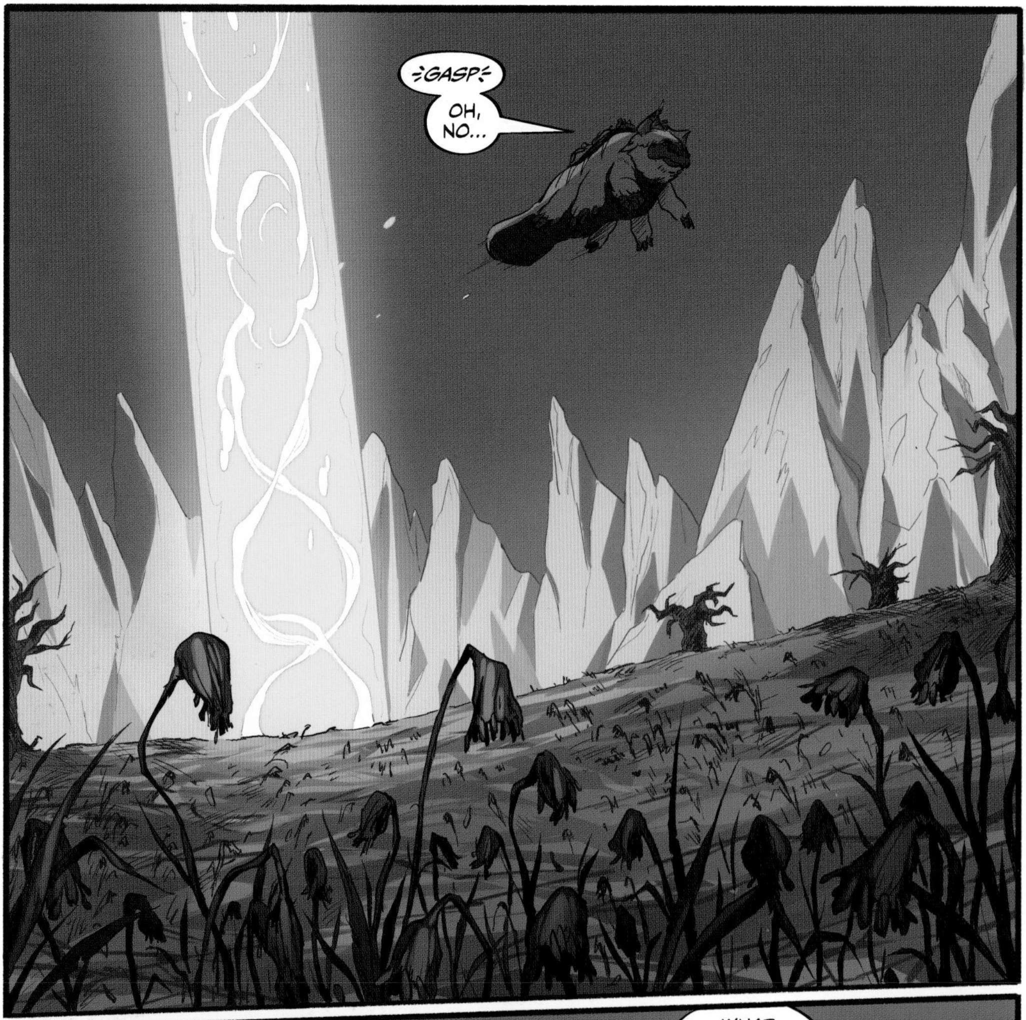
GASP
OH, NO...

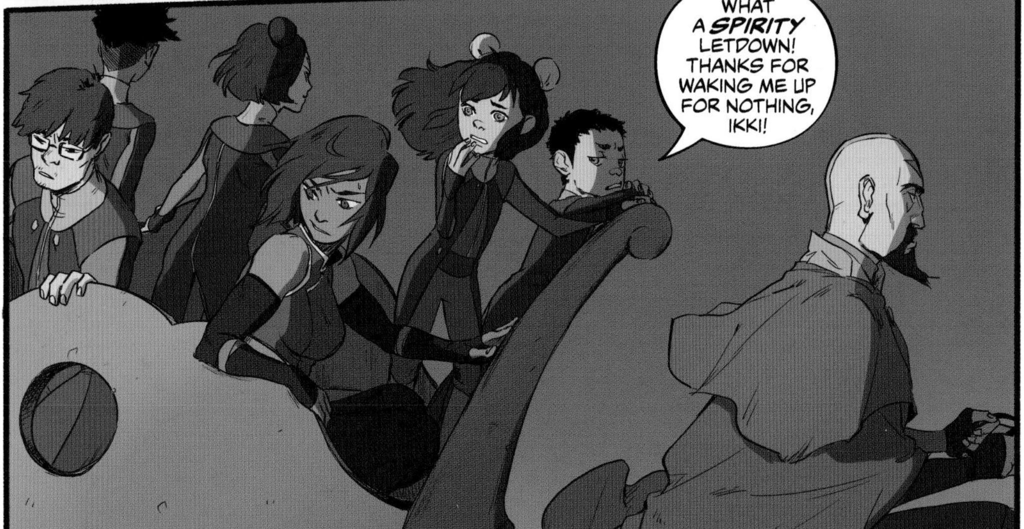
WHAT A SPIRITY LETDOWN! THANKS FOR WAKING ME UP FOR NOTHING, IKKI!

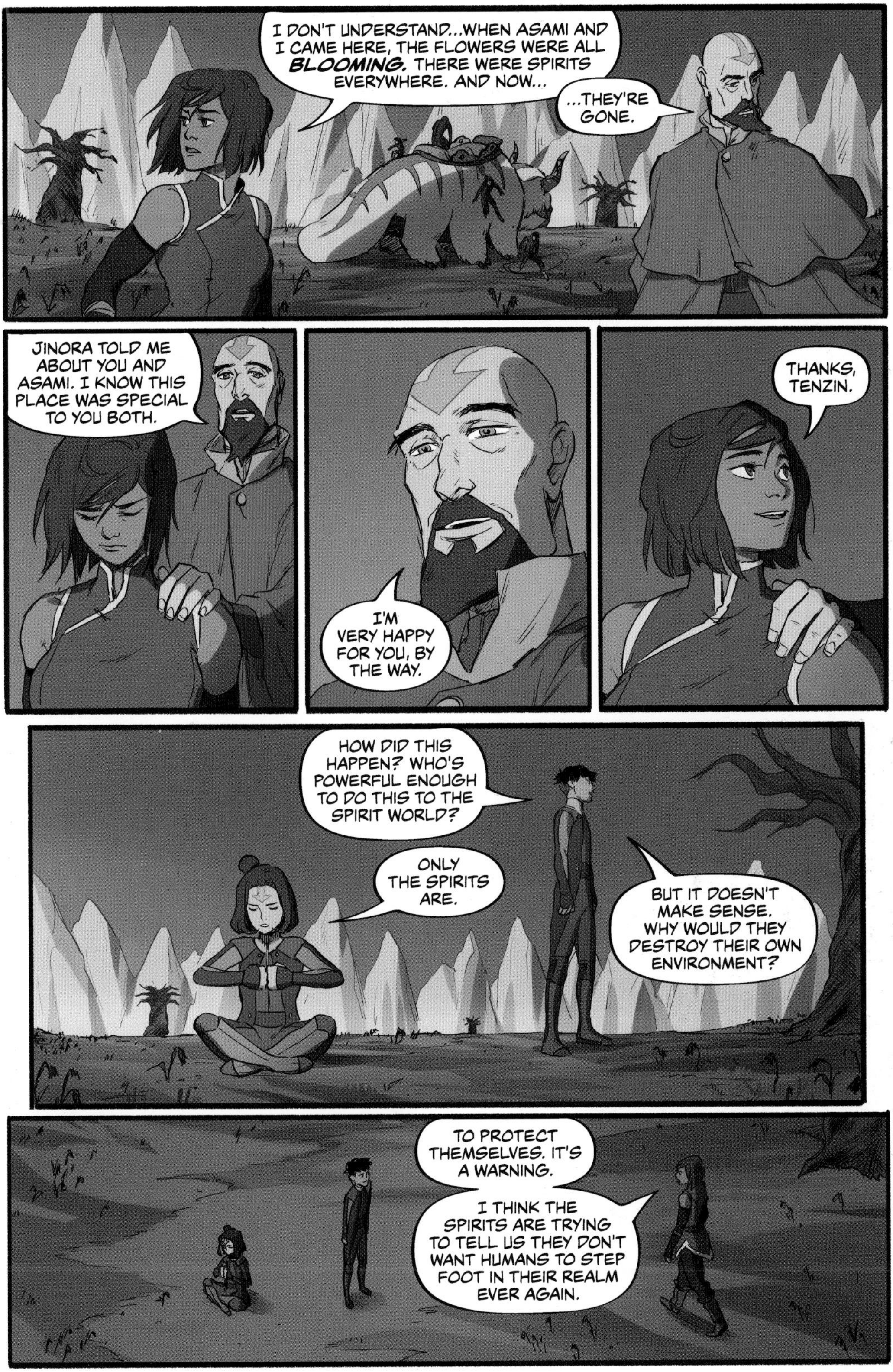
I DON'T UNDERSTAND...WHEN ASAMI AND I CAME HERE, THE FLOWERS WERE ALL BLOOMING. THERE WERE SPIRITS EVERYWHERE. AND NOW...
...THEY'RE GONE.
JINORA TOLD ME ABOUT YOU AND ASAMI. I KNOW THIS PLACE WAS SPECIAL TO YOU BOTH.
I'M VERY HAPPY FOR YOU, BY THE WAY.
THANKS, TENZIN.
HOW DID THIS HAPPEN? WHO'S POWERFUL ENOUGH TO DO THIS TO THE SPIRIT WORLD?
ONLY THE SPIRITS ARE.
BUT IT DOESN'T MAKE SENSE. WHY WOULD THEY DESTROY THEIR OWN ENVIRONMENT?
TO PROTECT THEMSELVES. IT'S A WARNING.
I THINK THE SPIRITS ARE TRYING TO TELL US THEY DON'T WANT HUMANS TO STEP FOOT IN THEIR REALM EVER AGAIN.

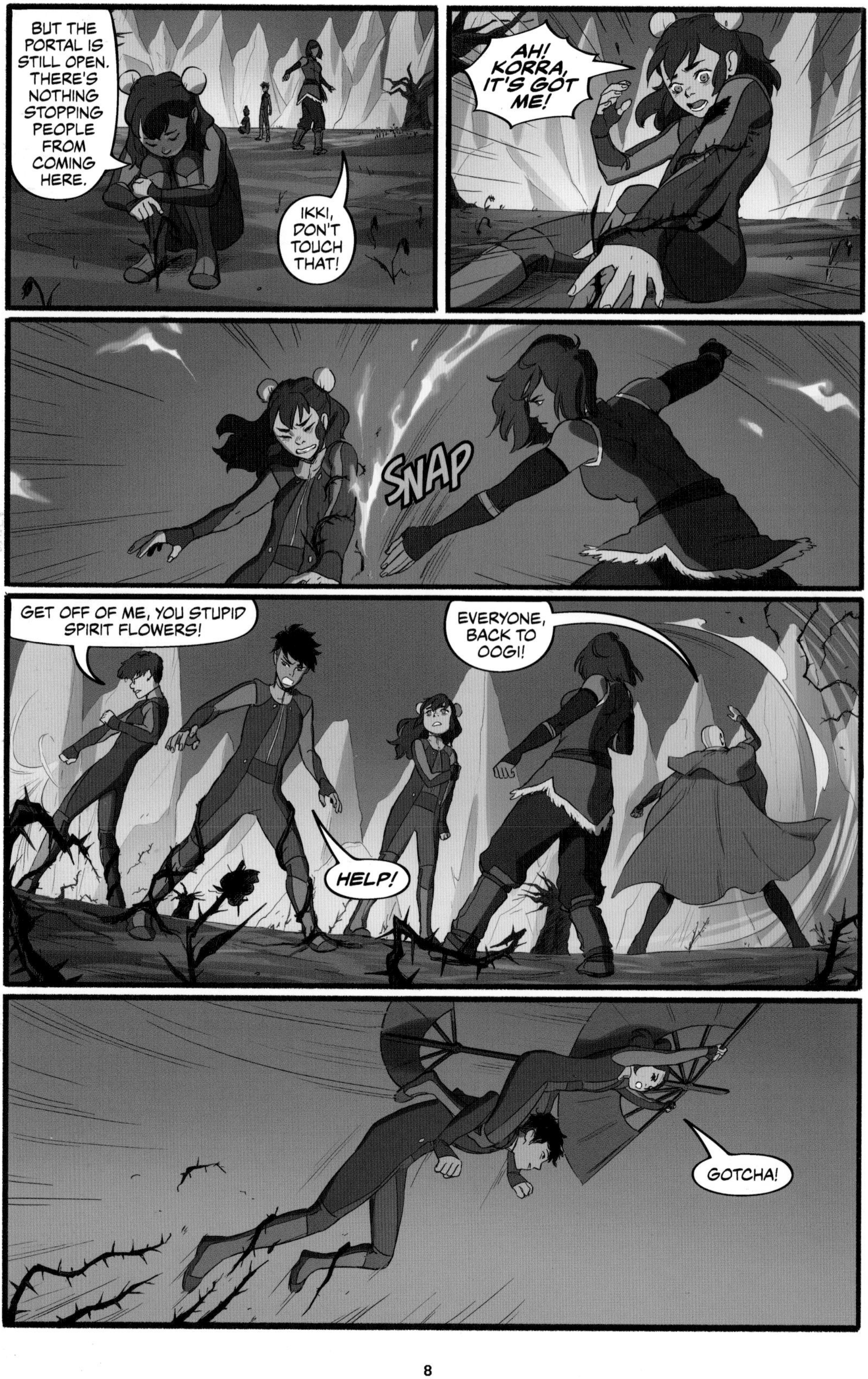

BUT THE PORTAL IS STILL OPEN. THERE'S NOTHING STOPPING PEOPLE FROM COMING HERE.
IKKI, DON'T TOUCH THAT!
AH! KORRA, IT'S GOT ME!
SNAP
GET OFF OF ME, YOU STUPID SPIRIT FLOWERS!
EVERYONE, BACK TO OOGI!
HELP!
GOTCHA!

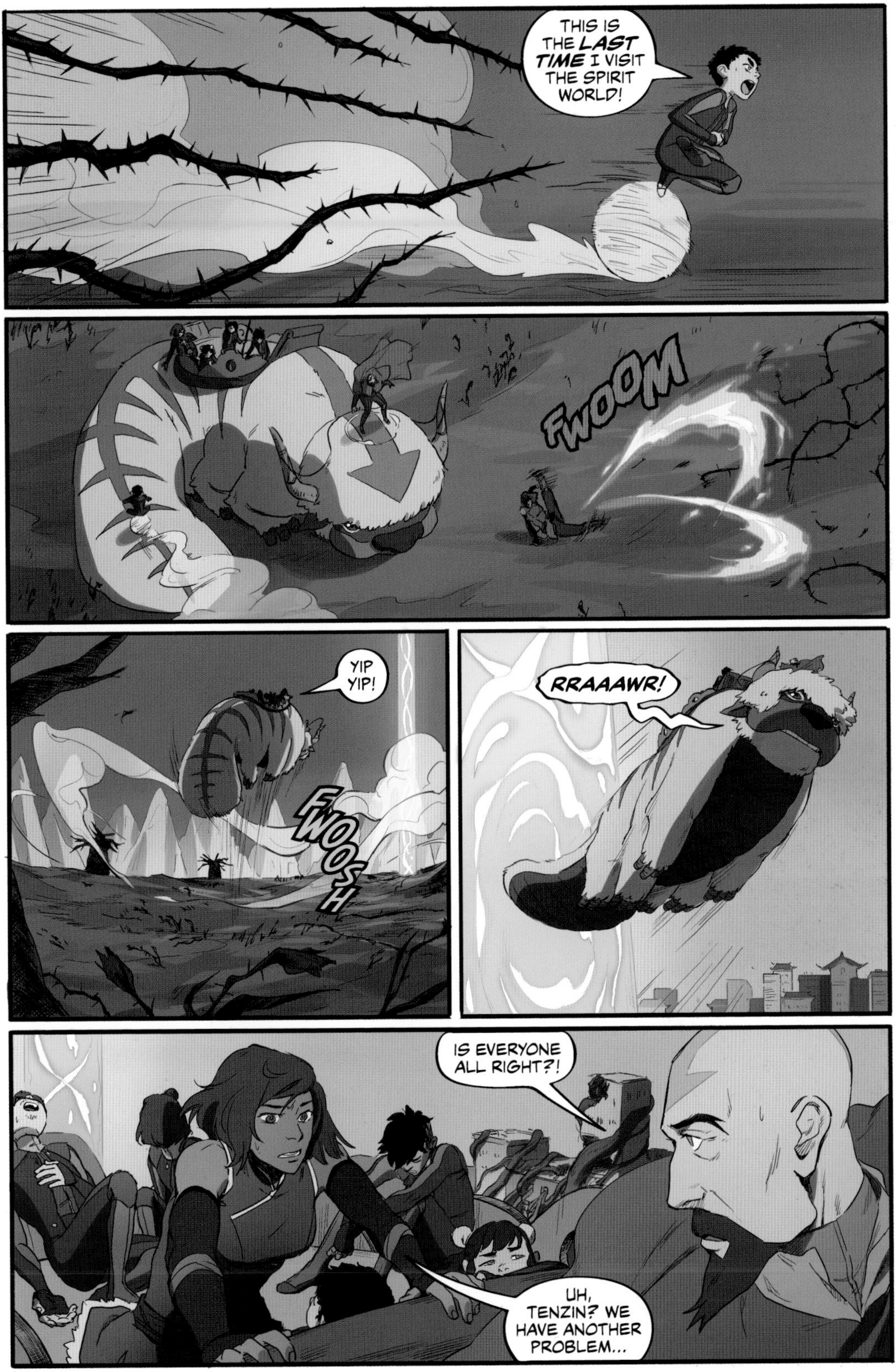
THIS IS THE LAST TIME I VISIT THE SPIRIT WORLD!
FWOOM
YIP YIP!
FWOOSH
RRAAAWR!
IS EVERYONE ALL RIGHT?!
UH, TENZIN? WE HAVE ANOTHER PROBLEM...

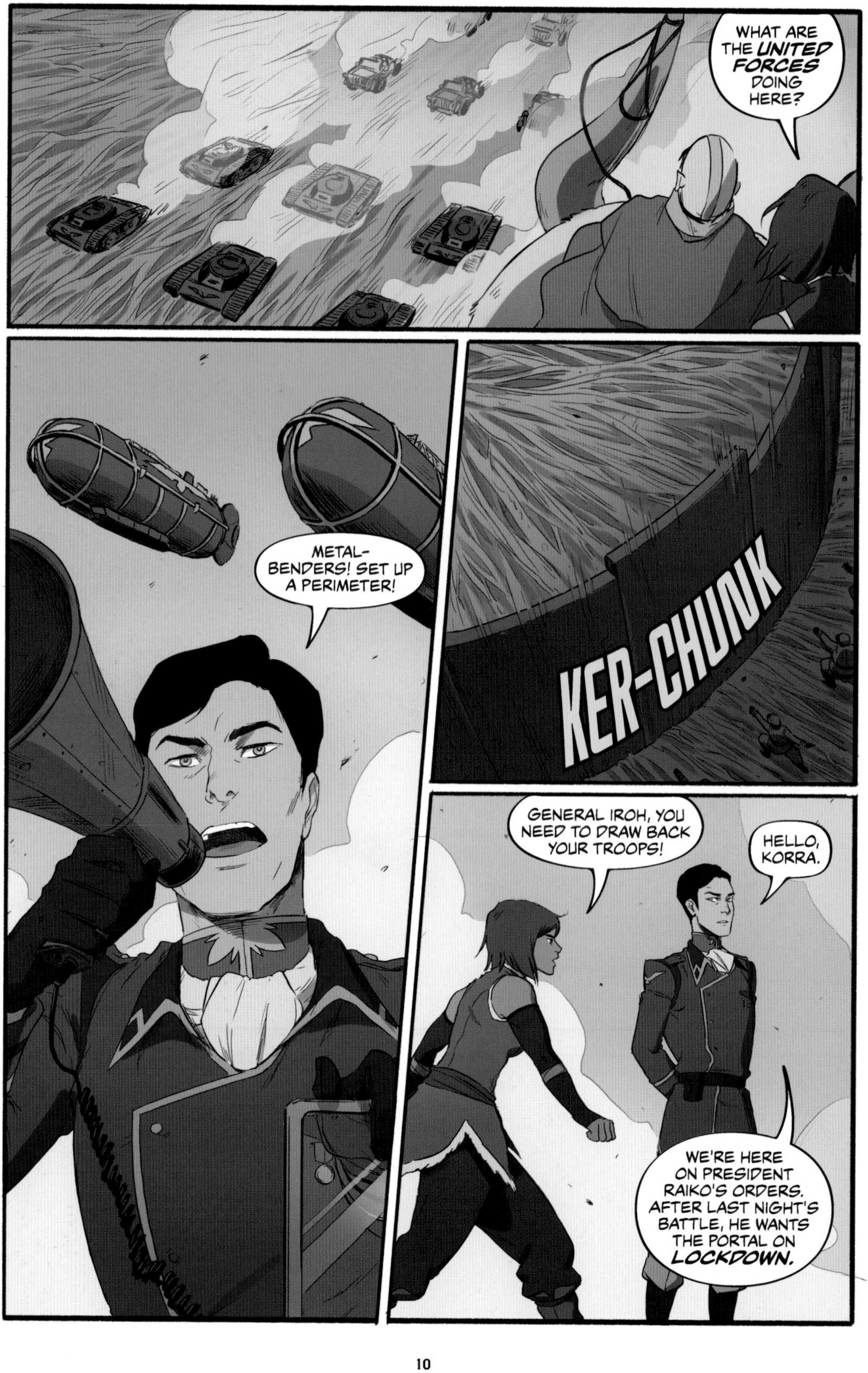
WHAT ARE THE UNITED FORCES DOING HERE?
METAL-BENDERS! SET UP A PERIMETER!
KER-CHUNK
GENERAL IROH, YOU NEED TO DRAW BACK YOUR TROOPS!
HELLO, KORRA.
WE'RE HERE ON PRESIDENT RAIKO'S ORDERS. AFTER LAST NIGHT'S BATTLE, HE WANTS THE PORTAL ON LOCKDOWN.

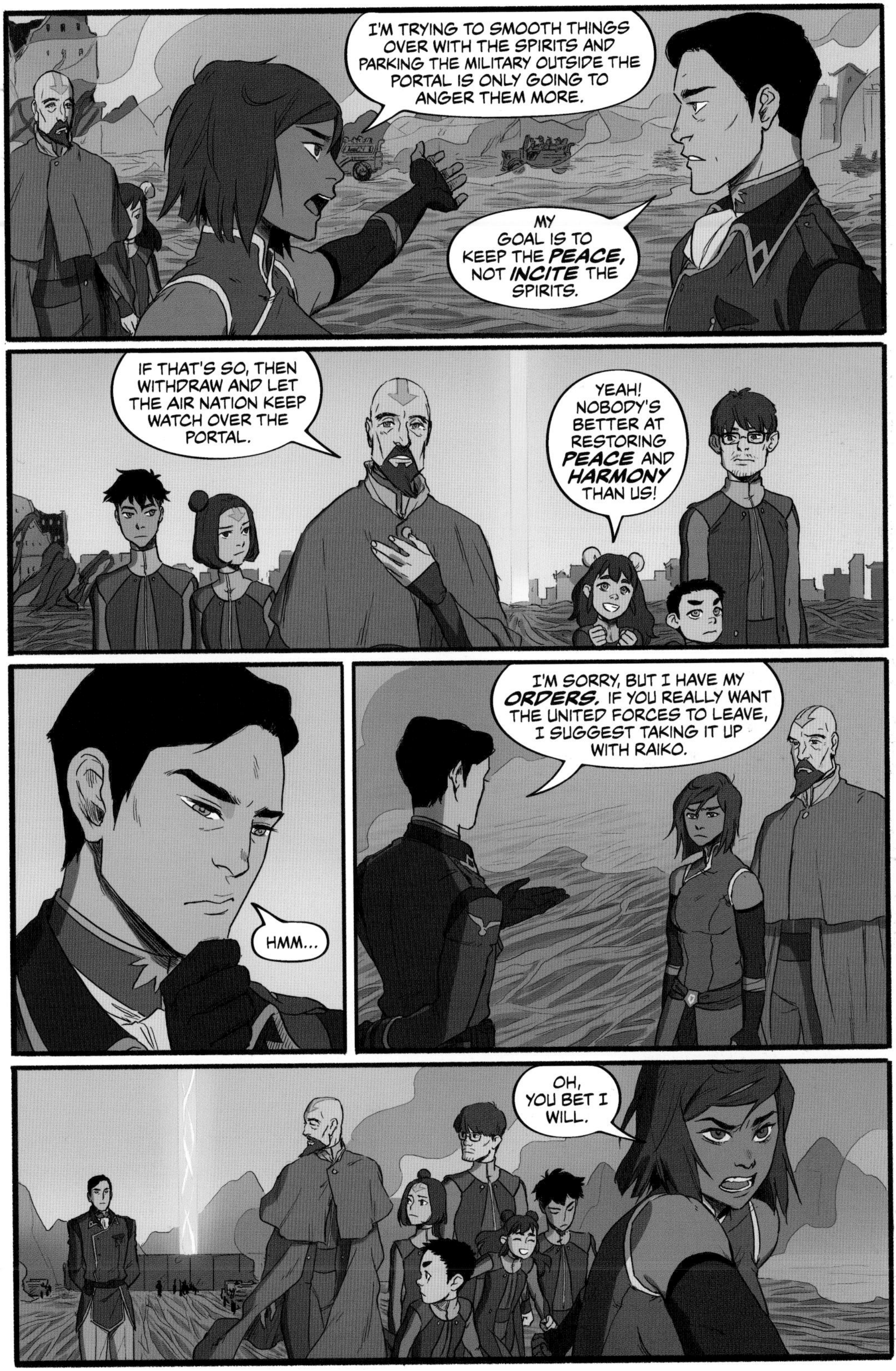
I'M TRYING TO SMOOTH THINGS OVER WITH THE SPIRITS AND PARKING THE MILITARY OUTSIDE THE PORTAL IS ONLY GOING TO ANGER THEM MORE.
MY GOAL IS TO KEEP THE PEACE, NOT INCITE THE SPIRITS.
IF THAT'S SO, THEN WITHDRAW AND LET THE AIR NATION KEEP WATCH OVER THE PORTAL.
YEAH! NOBODY'S BETTER AT RESTORING PEACE AND HARMONY THAN US!
HMM...
I'M SORRY, BUT I HAVE MY ORDERS. IF YOU REALLY WANT THE UNITED FORCES TO LEAVE, I SUGGEST TAKING IT UP WITH RAIKO.
OH, YOU BET I WILL.

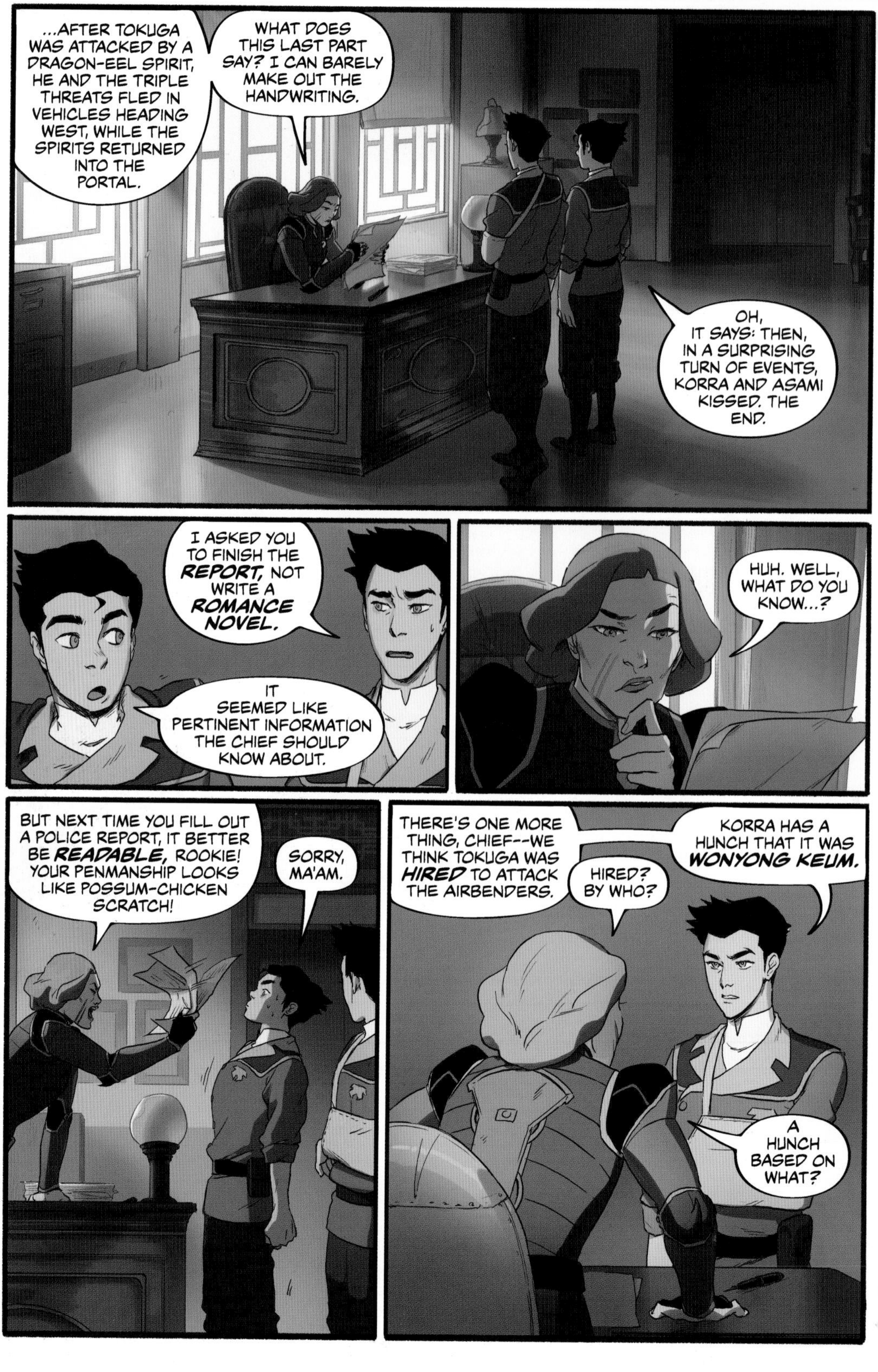
...AFTER TOKUGA WAS ATTACKED BY A DRAGON-EEL SPIRIT, HE AND THE TRIPLE THREATS FLED IN VEHICLES HEADING WEST, WHILE THE SPIRITS RETURNED INTO THE PORTAL.
WHAT DOES THIS LAST PART SAY? I CAN BARELY MAKE OUT THE HANDWRITING.
OH, IT SAYS: THEN, IN A SURPRISING TURN OF EVENTS, KORRA AND ASAMI KISSED. THE END.
I ASKED YOU TO FINISH THE ***REPORT,*** NOT WRITE A ***ROMANCE NOVEL.***
IT SEEMED LIKE PERTINENT INFORMATION THE CHIEF SHOULD KNOW ABOUT.
HUH. WELL, WHAT DO YOU KNOW...?
BUT NEXT TIME YOU FILL OUT A POLICE REPORT, IT BETTER BE ***READABLE,*** ROOKIE! YOUR PENMANSHIP LOOKS LIKE POSSUM-CHICKEN SCRATCH!
SORRY, MA'AM.
THERE'S ONE MORE THING, CHIEF--WE THINK TOKUGA WAS ***HIRED*** TO ATTACK THE AIRBENDERS.
HIRED? BY WHO?
KORRA HAS A HUNCH THAT IT WAS ***WONYONG KEUM.***
A HUNCH BASED ON WHAT?

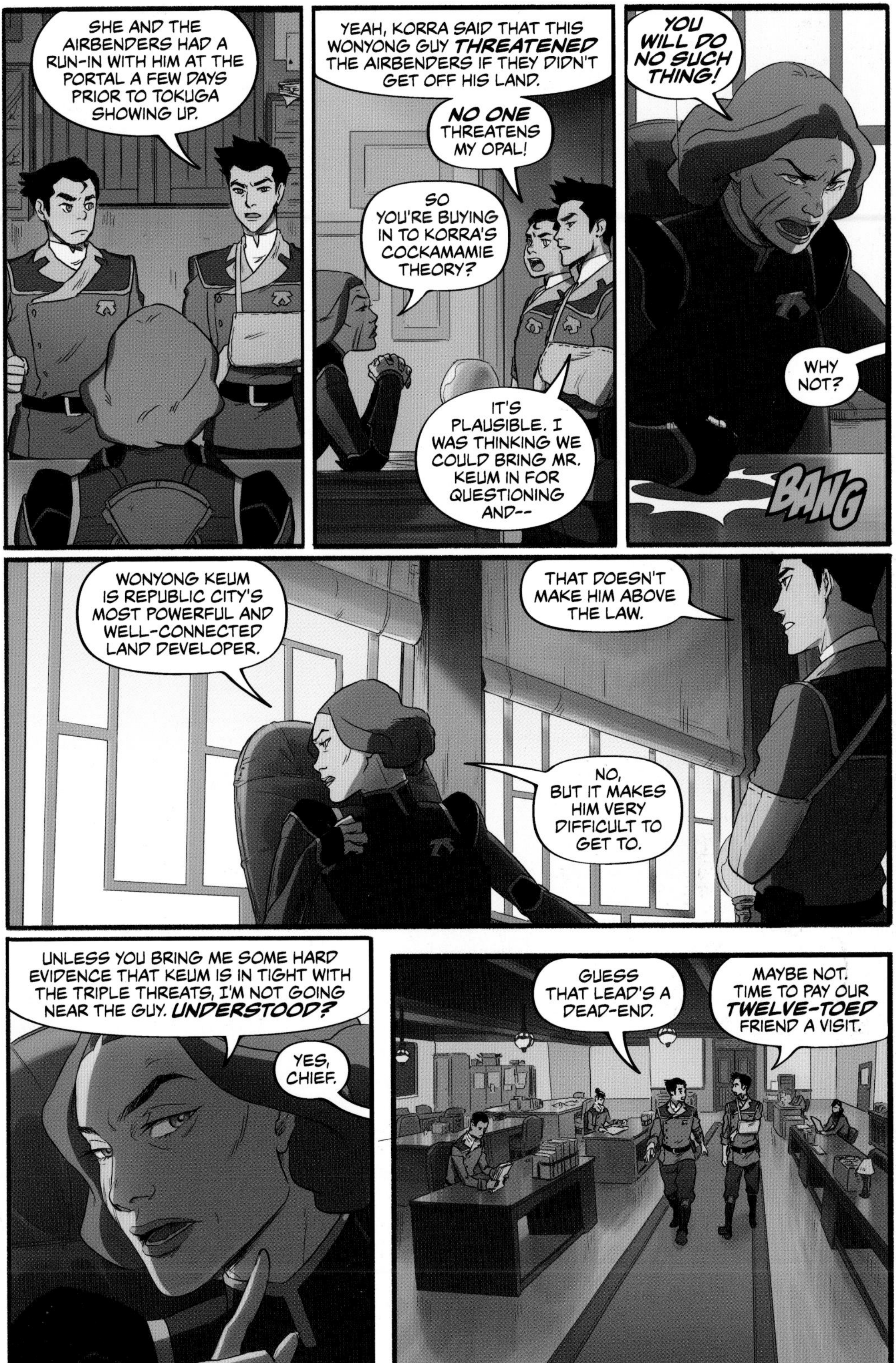
SHE AND THE AIRBENDERS HAD A RUN-IN WITH HIM AT THE PORTAL A FEW DAYS PRIOR TO TOKUGA SHOWING UP.
YEAH, KORRA SAID THAT THIS WONYONG GUY **THREATENED** THE AIRBENDERS IF THEY DIDN'T GET OFF HIS LAND.
NO ONE THREATENS MY OPAL!
SO YOU'RE BUYING IN TO KORRA'S COCKAMAMIE THEORY?
IT'S PLAUSIBLE. I WAS THINKING WE COULD BRING MR. KEUM IN FOR QUESTIONING AND--
YOU WILL DO NO SUCH THING!
WHY NOT?
BANG
WONYONG KEUM IS REPUBLIC CITY'S MOST POWERFUL AND WELL-CONNECTED LAND DEVELOPER.
THAT DOESN'T MAKE HIM ABOVE THE LAW.
NO, BUT IT MAKES HIM VERY DIFFICULT TO GET TO.
UNLESS YOU BRING ME SOME HARD EVIDENCE THAT KEUM IS IN TIGHT WITH THE TRIPLE THREATS, I'M NOT GOING NEAR THE GUY. **UNDERSTOOD?**
YES, CHIEF.
GUESS THAT LEAD'S A DEAD-END.
MAYBE NOT. TIME TO PAY OUR **TWELVE-TOED** FRIEND A VISIT.

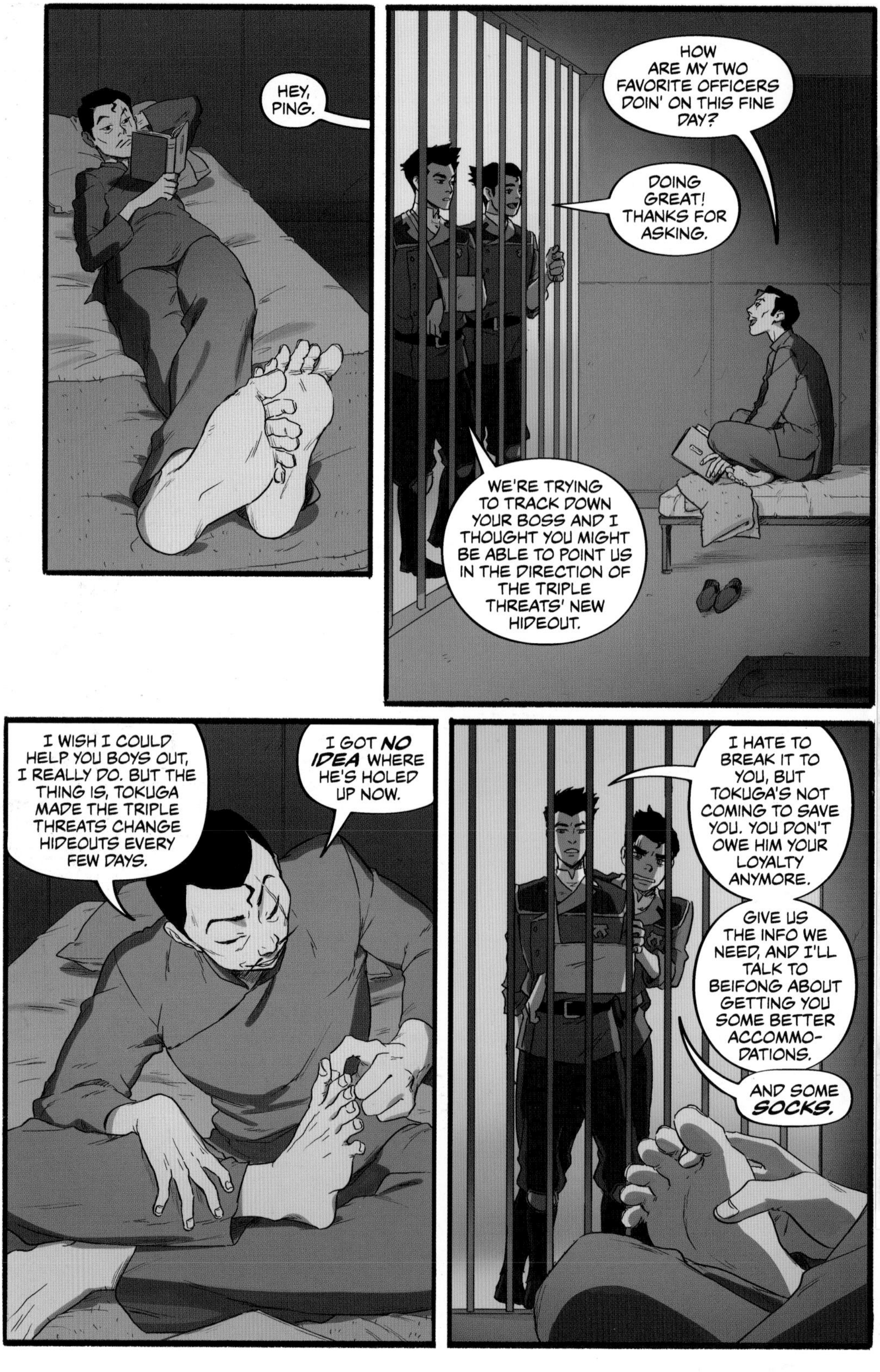
HEY, PING.
HOW ARE MY TWO FAVORITE OFFICERS DOIN' ON THIS FINE DAY?
DOING GREAT! THANKS FOR ASKING.
WE'RE TRYING TO TRACK DOWN YOUR BOSS AND I THOUGHT YOU MIGHT BE ABLE TO POINT US IN THE DIRECTION OF THE TRIPLE THREATS' NEW HIDEOUT.
I WISH I COULD HELP YOU BOYS OUT, I REALLY DO. BUT THE THING IS, TOKUGA MADE THE TRIPLE THREATS CHANGE HIDEOUTS EVERY FEW DAYS.
I GOT ***NO IDEA*** WHERE HE'S HOLED UP NOW.
I HATE TO BREAK IT TO YOU, BUT TOKUGA'S NOT COMING TO SAVE YOU. YOU DON'T OWE HIM YOUR LOYALTY ANYMORE.
GIVE US THE INFO WE NEED, AND I'LL TALK TO BEIFONG ABOUT GETTING YOU SOME BETTER ACCOMMO-DATIONS.
AND SOME ***SOCKS.***

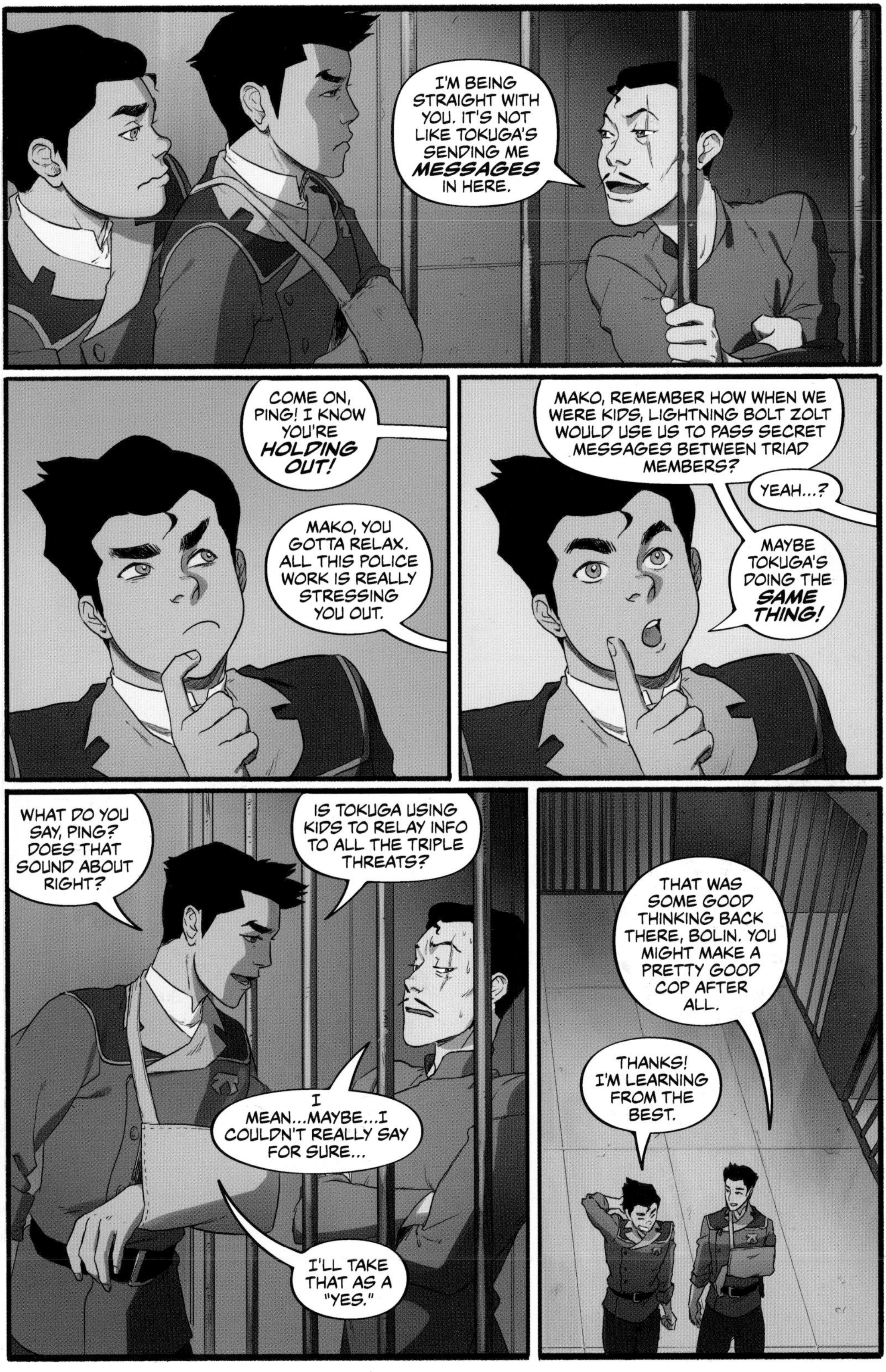
I'M BEING STRAIGHT WITH YOU. IT'S NOT LIKE TOKUGA'S SENDING ME MESSAGES IN HERE.
COME ON, PING! I KNOW YOU'RE HOLDING OUT!
MAKO, YOU GOTTA RELAX. ALL THIS POLICE WORK IS REALLY STRESSING YOU OUT.
MAKO, REMEMBER HOW WHEN WE WERE KIDS, LIGHTNING BOLT ZOLT WOULD USE US TO PASS SECRET MESSAGES BETWEEN TRIAD MEMBERS?
YEAH...?
MAYBE TOKUGA'S DOING THE SAME THING!
WHAT DO YOU SAY, PING? DOES THAT SOUND ABOUT RIGHT?
IS TOKUGA USING KIDS TO RELAY INFO TO ALL THE TRIPLE THREATS?
I MEAN...MAYBE...I COULDN'T REALLY SAY FOR SURE...
I'LL TAKE THAT AS A "YES."
THAT WAS SOME GOOD THINKING BACK THERE, BOLIN. YOU MIGHT MAKE A PRETTY GOOD COP AFTER ALL.
THANKS! I'M LEARNING FROM THE BEST.

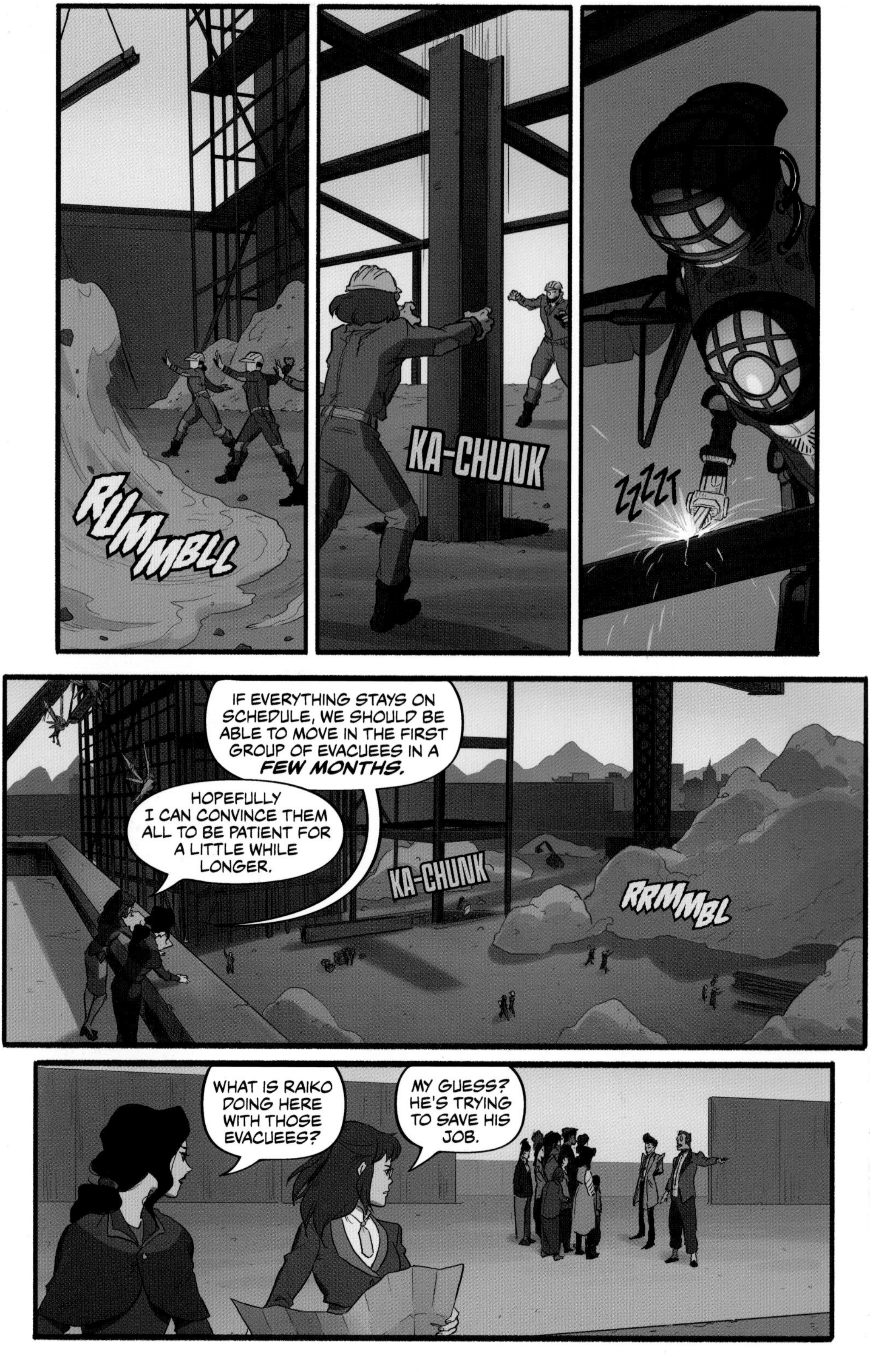
RUMMBLL
KA-CHUNK
ZZZZT
IF EVERYTHING STAYS ON SCHEDULE, WE SHOULD BE ABLE TO MOVE IN THE FIRST GROUP OF EVACUEES IN A *FEW MONTHS.*
HOPEFULLY I CAN CONVINCE THEM ALL TO BE PATIENT FOR A LITTLE WHILE LONGER.
KA-CHUNK
RRMMBL
WHAT IS RAIKO DOING HERE WITH THOSE EVACUEES?
MY GUESS? HE'S TRYING TO SAVE HIS JOB.

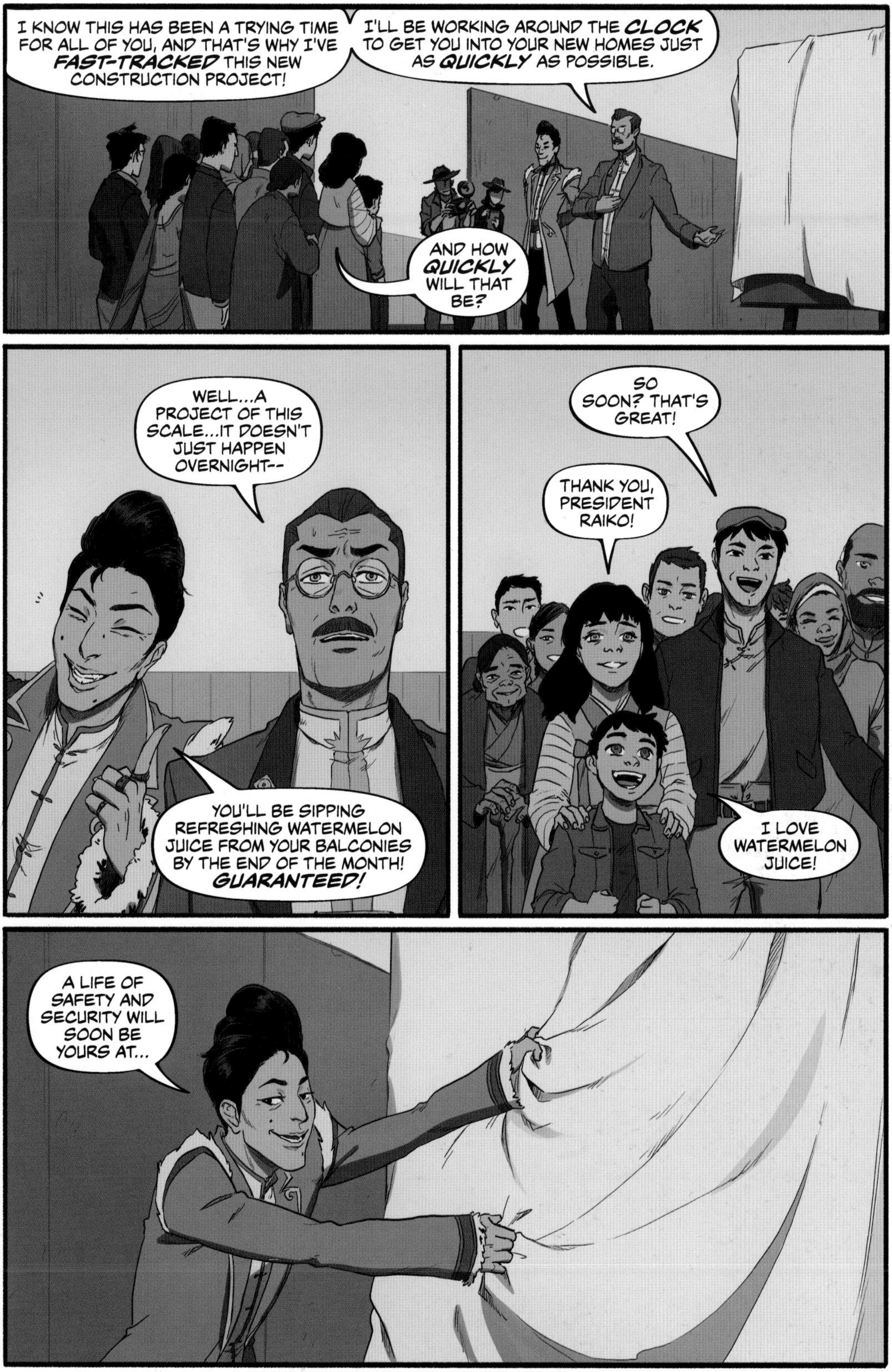
I KNOW THIS HAS BEEN A TRYING TIME FOR ALL OF YOU, AND THAT'S WHY I'VE *FAST-TRACKED* THIS NEW CONSTRUCTION PROJECT!
I'LL BE WORKING AROUND THE *CLOCK* TO GET YOU INTO YOUR NEW HOMES JUST AS *QUICKLY* AS POSSIBLE.
AND HOW *QUICKLY* WILL THAT BE?
WELL...A PROJECT OF THIS SCALE...IT DOESN'T JUST HAPPEN OVERNIGHT--
YOU'LL BE SIPPING REFRESHING WATERMELON JUICE FROM YOUR BALCONIES BY THE END OF THE MONTH! *GUARANTEED!*
SO SOON? THAT'S GREAT!
THANK YOU, PRESIDENT RAIKO!
I LOVE WATERMELON JUICE!
A LIFE OF SAFETY AND SECURITY WILL SOON BE YOURS AT...

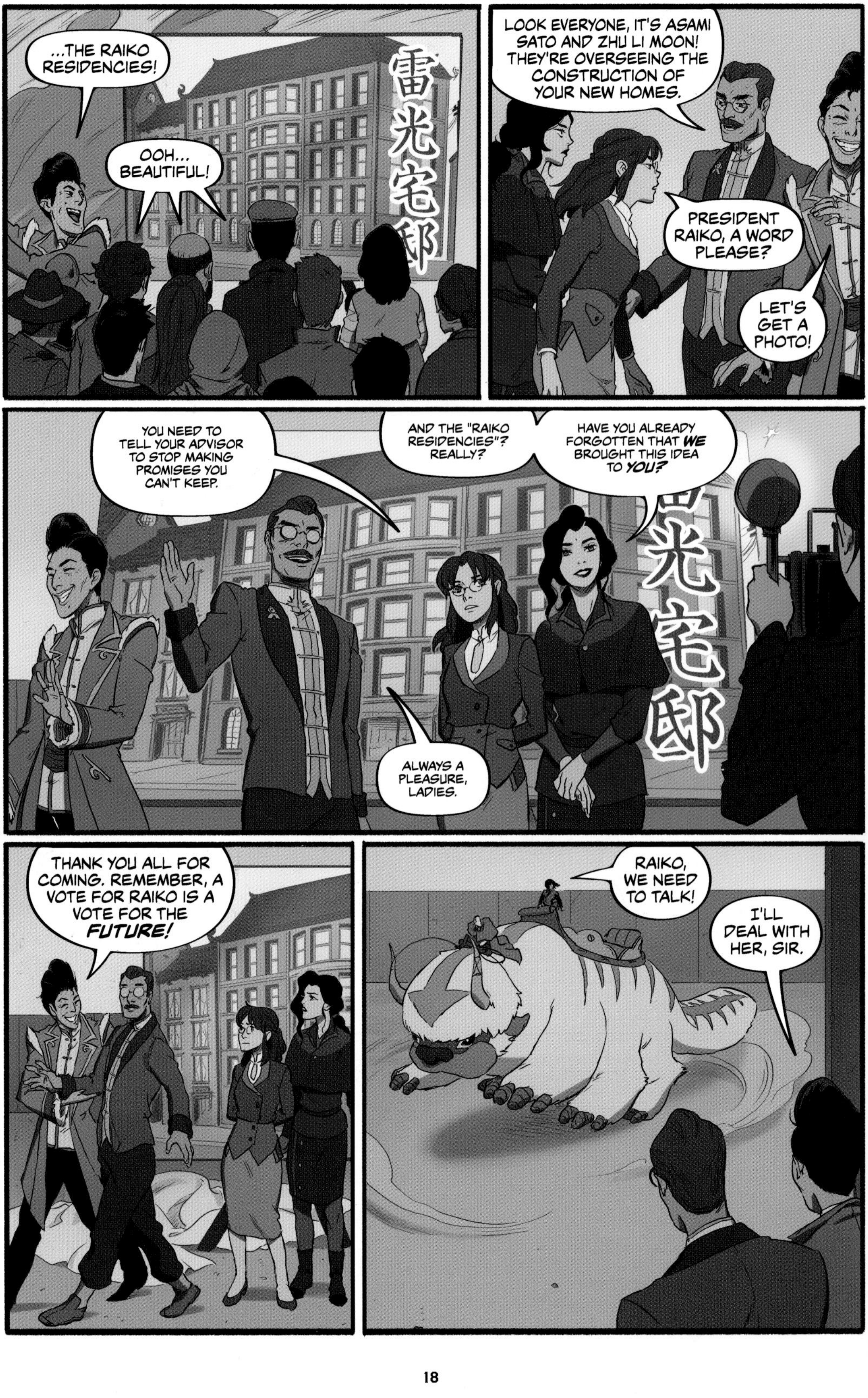
...THE RAIKO RESIDENCIES!
OOH... BEAUTIFUL!
雷光宅邸
LOOK EVERYONE, IT'S ASAMI SATO AND ZHU LI MOON! THEY'RE OVERSEEING THE CONSTRUCTION OF YOUR NEW HOMES.
PRESIDENT RAIKO, A WORD PLEASE?
LET'S GET A PHOTO!
YOU NEED TO TELL YOUR ADVISOR TO STOP MAKING PROMISES YOU CAN'T KEEP.
AND THE "RAIKO RESIDENCIES"? REALLY?
HAVE YOU ALREADY FORGOTTEN THAT *WE* BROUGHT THIS IDEA TO *YOU*?
ALWAYS A PLEASURE, LADIES.
THANK YOU ALL FOR COMING. REMEMBER, A VOTE FOR RAIKO IS A VOTE FOR THE *FUTURE!*
RAIKO, WE NEED TO TALK!
I'LL DEAL WITH HER, SIR.

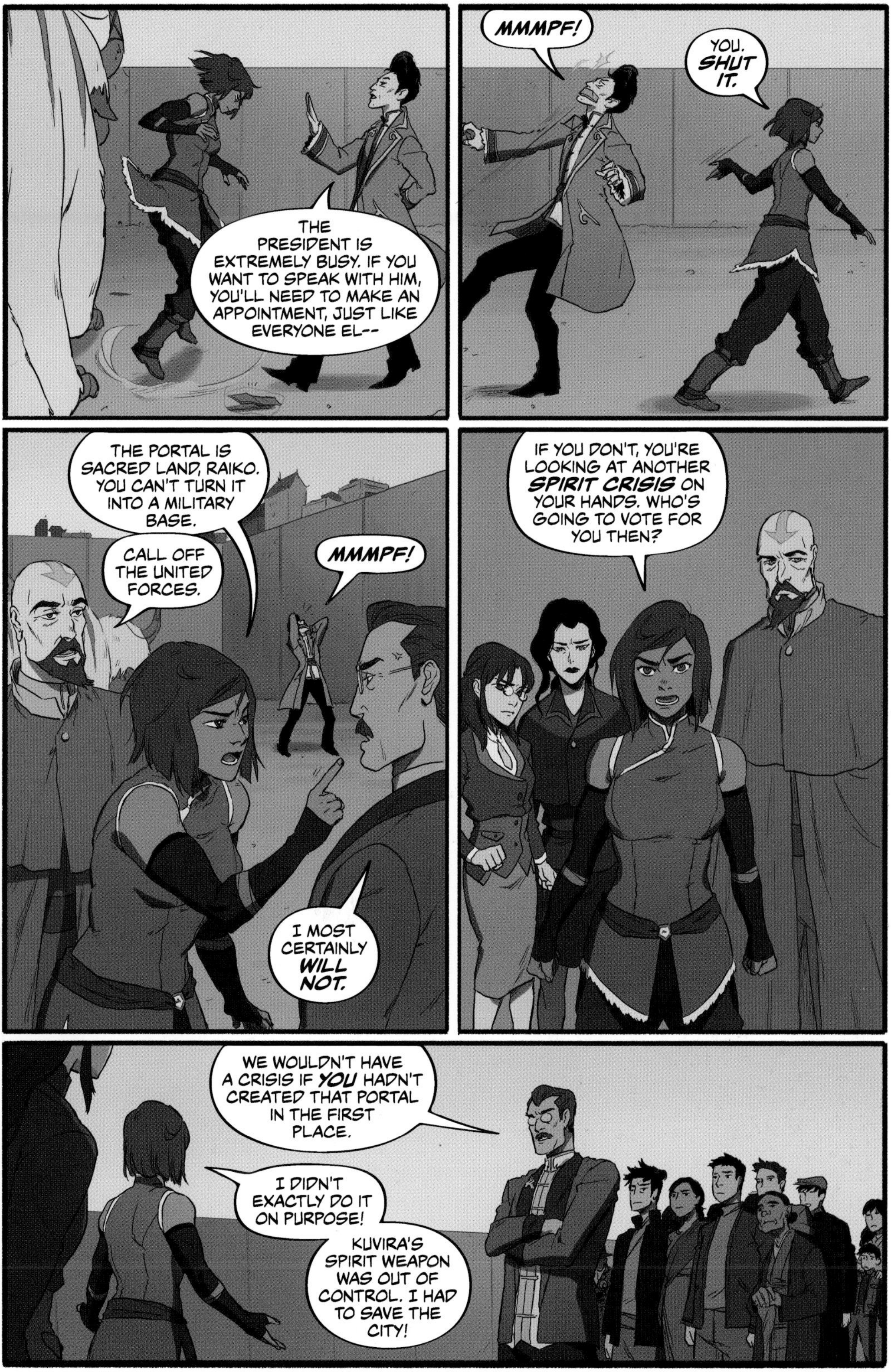
THE PRESIDENT IS EXTREMELY BUSY. IF YOU WANT TO SPEAK WITH HIM, YOU'LL NEED TO MAKE AN APPOINTMENT, JUST LIKE EVERYONE EL--
MMMPF!
YOU. SHUT IT.
THE PORTAL IS SACRED LAND, RAIKO. YOU CAN'T TURN IT INTO A MILITARY BASE.
CALL OFF THE UNITED FORCES.
MMMPF!
I MOST CERTAINLY WILL NOT.
IF YOU DON'T, YOU'RE LOOKING AT ANOTHER SPIRIT CRISIS ON YOUR HANDS. WHO'S GOING TO VOTE FOR YOU THEN?
WE WOULDN'T HAVE A CRISIS IF YOU HADN'T CREATED THAT PORTAL IN THE FIRST PLACE.
I DIDN'T EXACTLY DO IT ON PURPOSE!
KUVIRA'S SPIRIT WEAPON WAS OUT OF CONTROL. I HAD TO SAVE THE CITY!

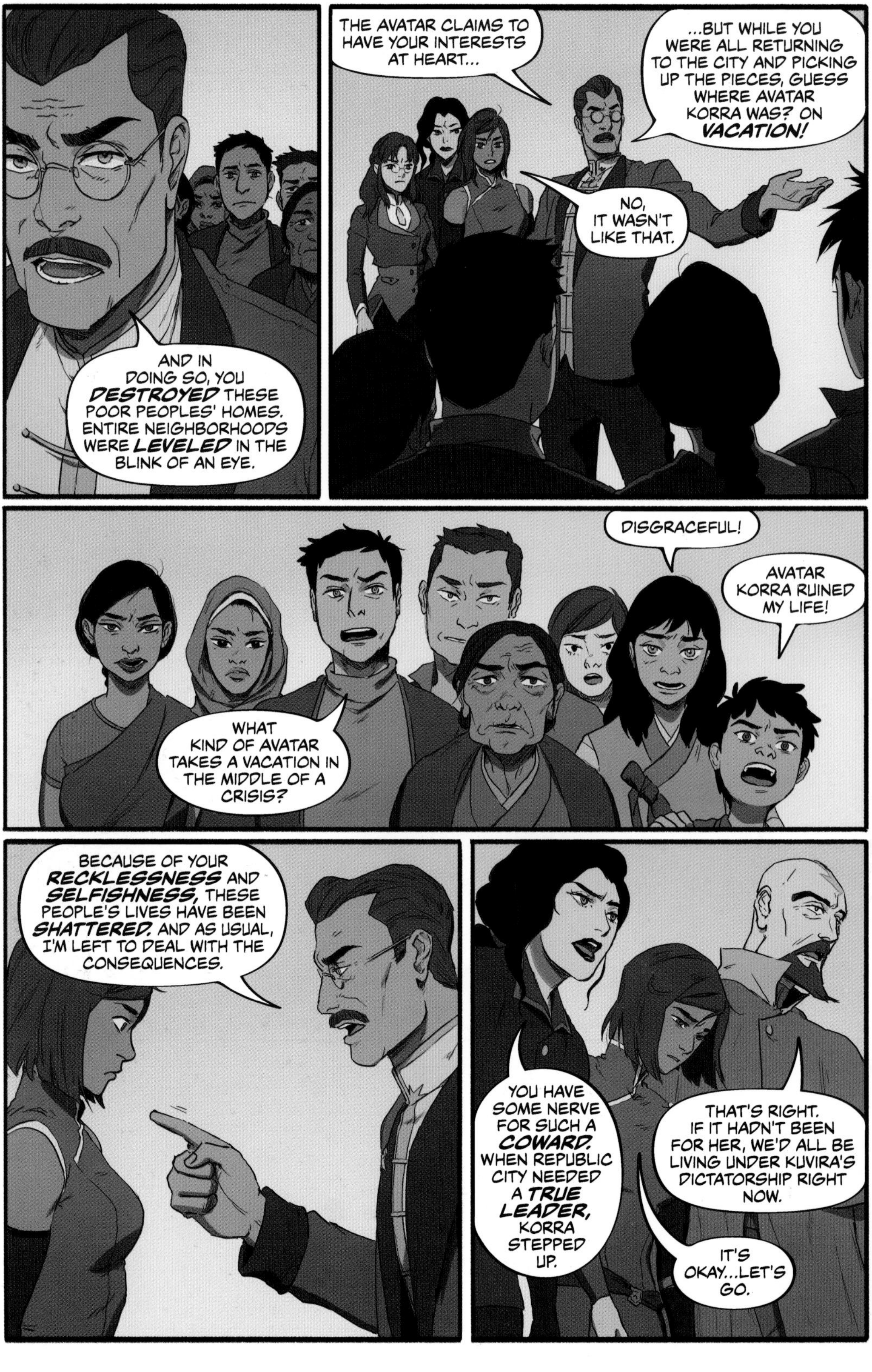
AND IN DOING SO, YOU DESTROYED THESE POOR PEOPLES' HOMES. ENTIRE NEIGHBORHOODS WERE LEVELED IN THE BLINK OF AN EYE.
THE AVATAR CLAIMS TO HAVE YOUR INTERESTS AT HEART...
...BUT WHILE YOU WERE ALL RETURNING TO THE CITY AND PICKING UP THE PIECES, GUESS WHERE AVATAR KORRA WAS? ON VACATION!
NO, IT WASN'T LIKE THAT.
DISGRACEFUL!
AVATAR KORRA RUINED MY LIFE!
WHAT KIND OF AVATAR TAKES A VACATION IN THE MIDDLE OF A CRISIS?
BECAUSE OF YOUR RECKLESSNESS AND SELFISHNESS, THESE PEOPLE'S LIVES HAVE BEEN SHATTERED. AND AS USUAL, I'M LEFT TO DEAL WITH THE CONSEQUENCES.
YOU HAVE SOME NERVE FOR SUCH A COWARD. WHEN REPUBLIC CITY NEEDED A TRUE LEADER, KORRA STEPPED UP.
THAT'S RIGHT. IF IT HADN'T BEEN FOR HER, WE'D ALL BE LIVING UNDER KUVIRA'S DICTATORSHIP RIGHT NOW.
IT'S OKAY...LET'S GO.

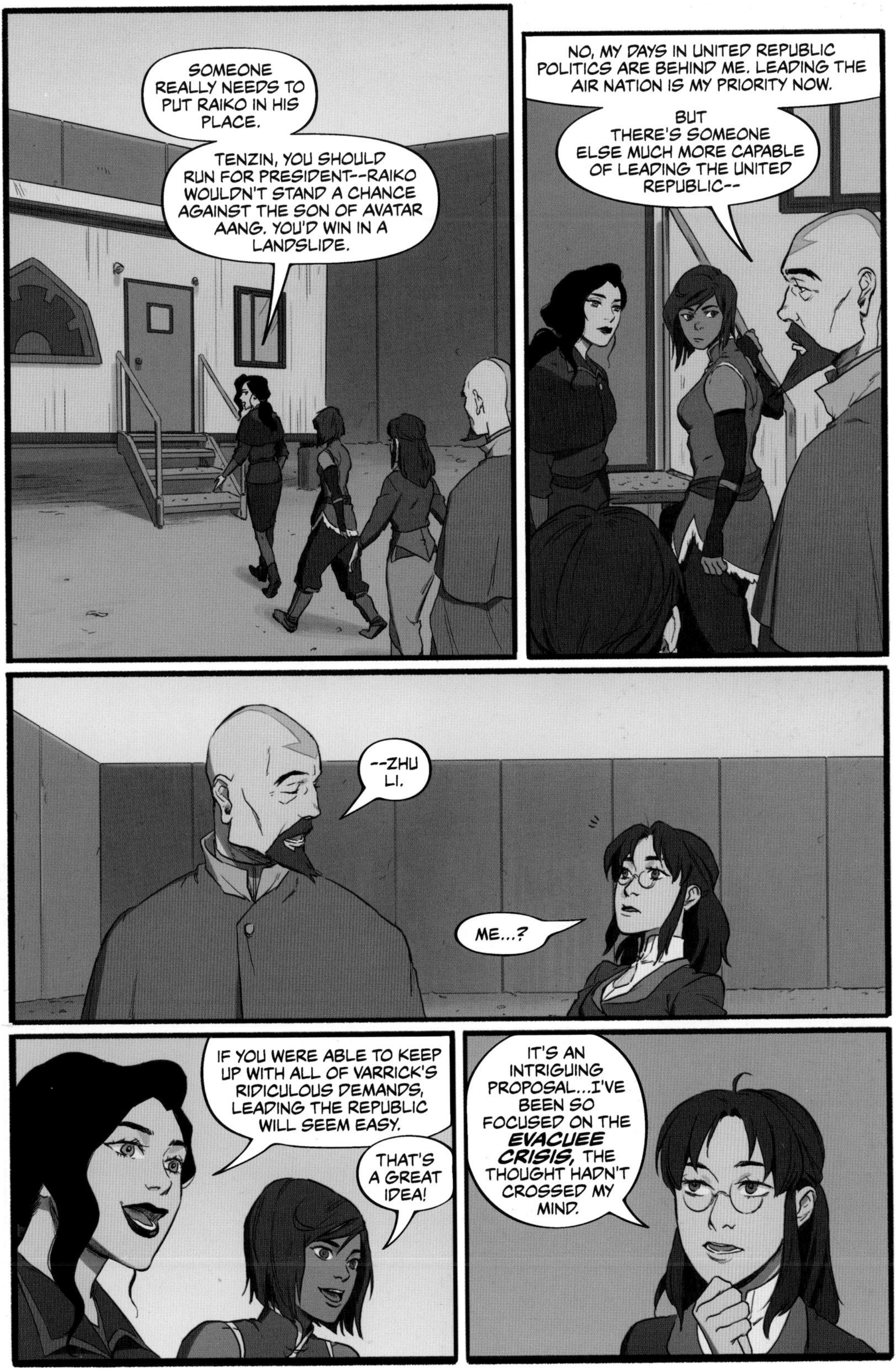
SOMEONE REALLY NEEDS TO PUT RAIKO IN HIS PLACE.
TENZIN, YOU SHOULD RUN FOR PRESIDENT--RAIKO WOULDN'T STAND A CHANCE AGAINST THE SON OF AVATAR AANG. YOU'D WIN IN A LANDSLIDE.
NO, MY DAYS IN UNITED REPUBLIC POLITICS ARE BEHIND ME. LEADING THE AIR NATION IS MY PRIORITY NOW.
BUT THERE'S SOMEONE ELSE MUCH MORE CAPABLE OF LEADING THE UNITED REPUBLIC--
--ZHU LI.
ME...?
IF YOU WERE ABLE TO KEEP UP WITH ALL OF VARRICK'S RIDICULOUS DEMANDS, LEADING THE REPUBLIC WILL SEEM EASY.
THAT'S A GREAT IDEA!
IT'S AN INTRIGUING PROPOSAL...I'VE BEEN SO FOCUSED ON THE ***EVACUEE CRISIS,*** THE THOUGHT HADN'T CROSSED MY MIND.

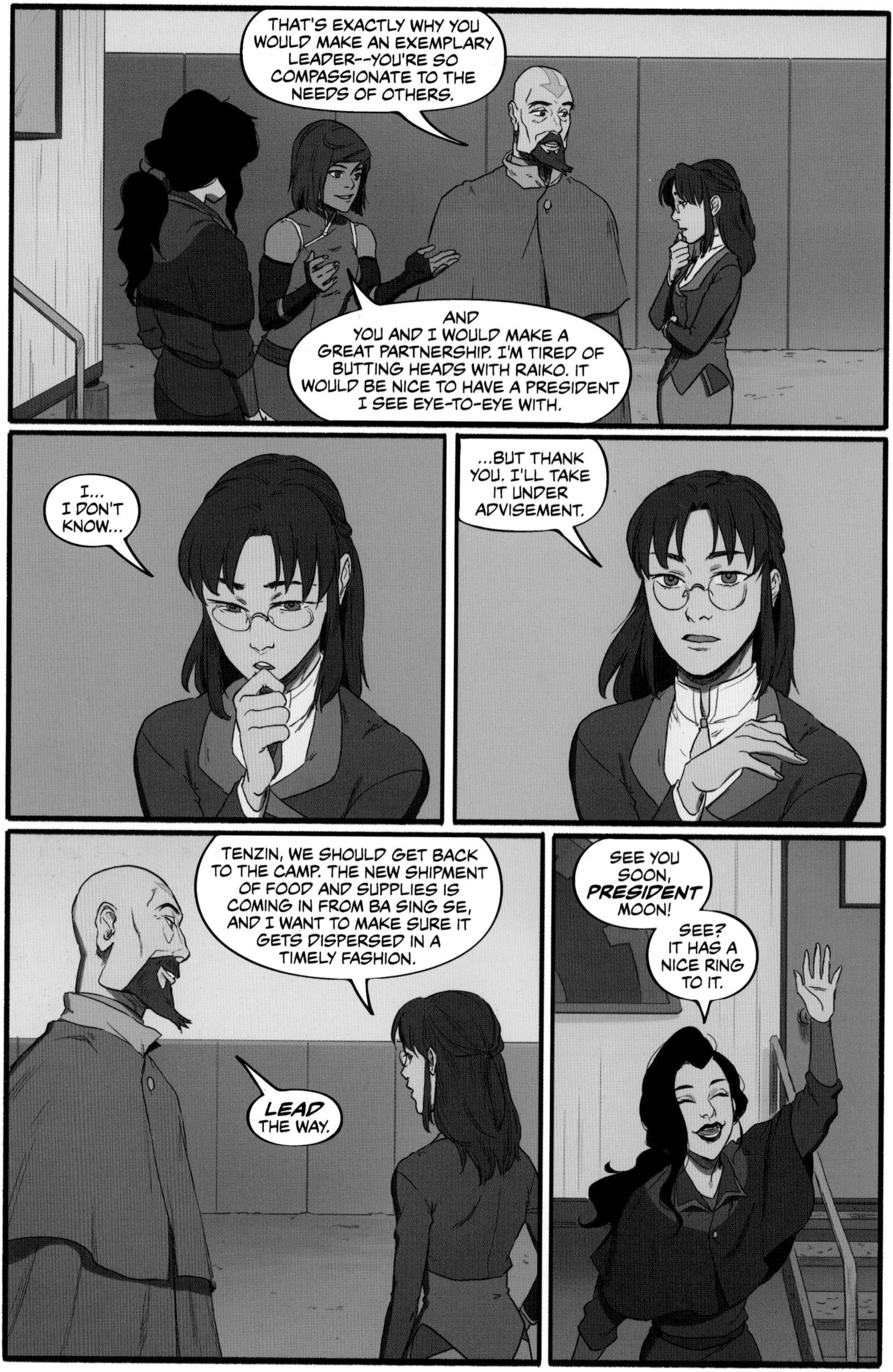
THAT'S EXACTLY WHY YOU WOULD MAKE AN EXEMPLARY LEADER--YOU'RE SO COMPASSIONATE TO THE NEEDS OF OTHERS.
AND YOU AND I WOULD MAKE A GREAT PARTNERSHIP. I'M TIRED OF BUTTING HEADS WITH RAIKO. IT WOULD BE NICE TO HAVE A PRESIDENT I SEE EYE-TO-EYE WITH.
I... I DON'T KNOW...
...BUT THANK YOU. I'LL TAKE IT UNDER ADVISEMENT.
TENZIN, WE SHOULD GET BACK TO THE CAMP. THE NEW SHIPMENT OF FOOD AND SUPPLIES IS COMING IN FROM BA SING SE, AND I WANT TO MAKE SURE IT GETS DISPERSED IN A TIMELY FASHION.
LEAD THE WAY.
SEE YOU SOON, PRESIDENT MOON!
SEE? IT HAS A NICE RING TO IT.

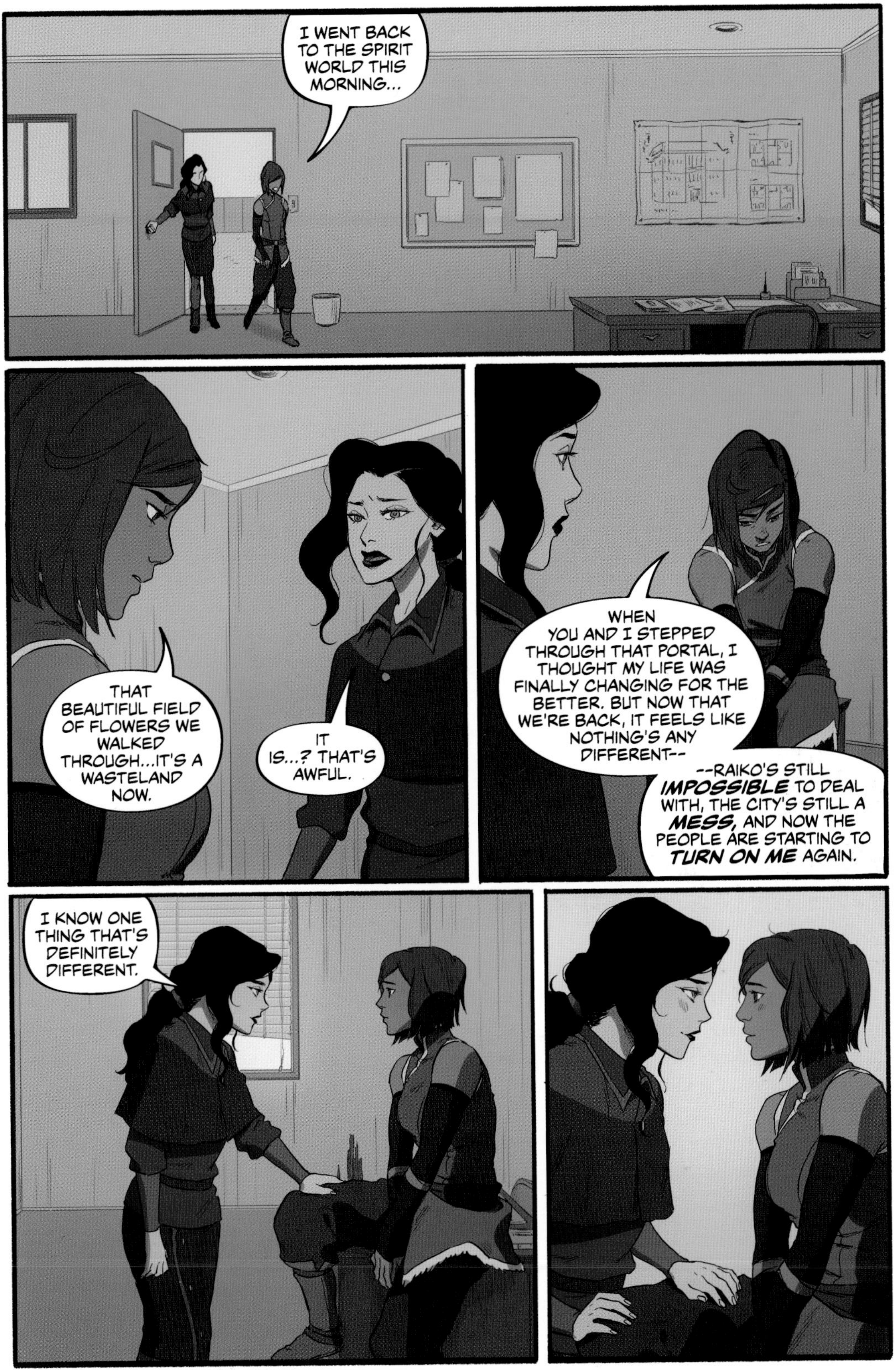
I WENT BACK TO THE SPIRIT WORLD THIS MORNING...
THAT BEAUTIFUL FIELD OF FLOWERS WE WALKED THROUGH...IT'S A WASTELAND NOW.
IT IS...? THAT'S AWFUL.
WHEN YOU AND I STEPPED THROUGH THAT PORTAL, I THOUGHT MY LIFE WAS FINALLY CHANGING FOR THE BETTER. BUT NOW THAT WE'RE BACK, IT FEELS LIKE NOTHING'S ANY DIFFERENT--
--RAIKO'S STILL IMPOSSIBLE TO DEAL WITH, THE CITY'S STILL A MESS, AND NOW THE PEOPLE ARE STARTING TO TURN ON ME AGAIN.
I KNOW ONE THING THAT'S DEFINITELY DIFFERENT.

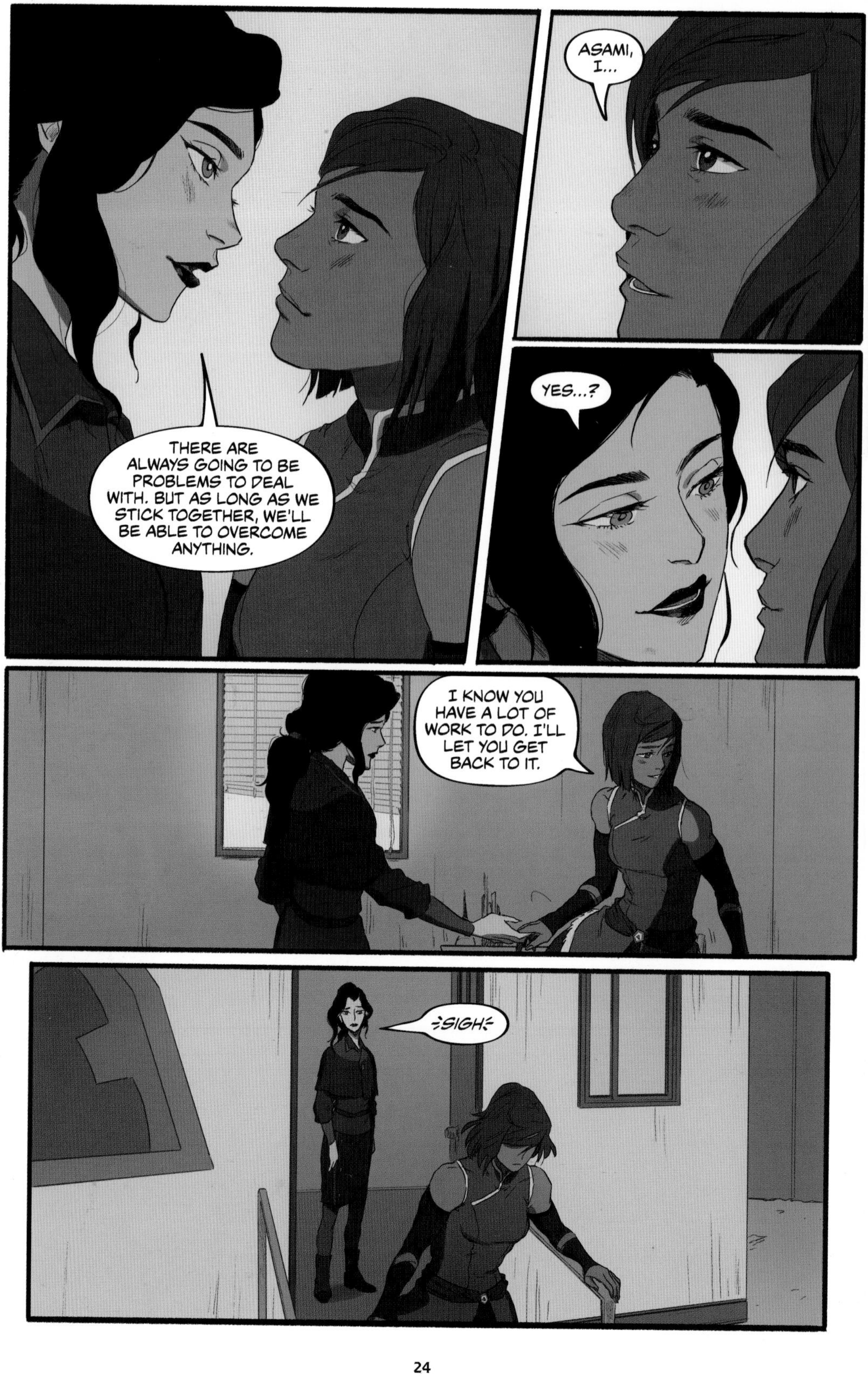
THERE ARE ALWAYS GOING TO BE PROBLEMS TO DEAL WITH. BUT AS LONG AS WE STICK TOGETHER, WE'LL BE ABLE TO OVERCOME ANYTHING.
ASAMI, I...
YES...?
I KNOW YOU HAVE A LOT OF WORK TO DO. I'LL LET YOU GET BACK TO IT.
SIGH

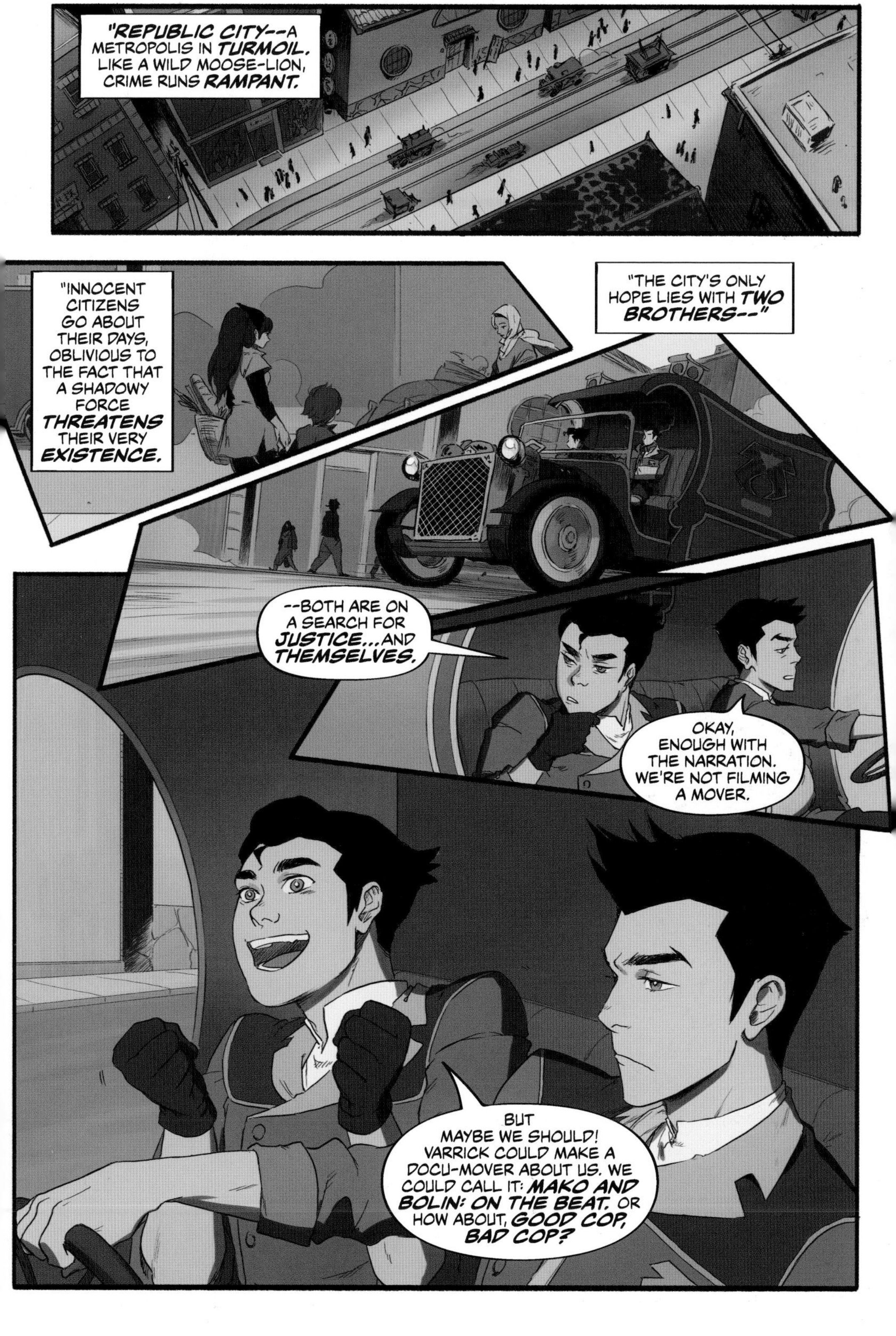
"REPUBLIC CITY--A METROPOLIS IN TURMOIL. LIKE A WILD MOOSE-LION, CRIME RUNS RAMPANT.
"INNOCENT CITIZENS GO ABOUT THEIR DAYS, OBLIVIOUS TO THE FACT THAT A SHADOWY FORCE THREATENS THEIR VERY EXISTENCE.
"THE CITY'S ONLY HOPE LIES WITH TWO BROTHERS--"
--BOTH ARE ON A SEARCH FOR JUSTICE...AND THEMSELVES.
OKAY, ENOUGH WITH THE NARRATION. WE'RE NOT FILMING A MOVER.
BUT MAYBE WE SHOULD! VARRICK COULD MAKE A DOCU-MOVER ABOUT US. WE COULD CALL IT: MAKO AND BOLIN: ON THE BEAT. OR HOW ABOUT, GOOD COP, BAD COP?

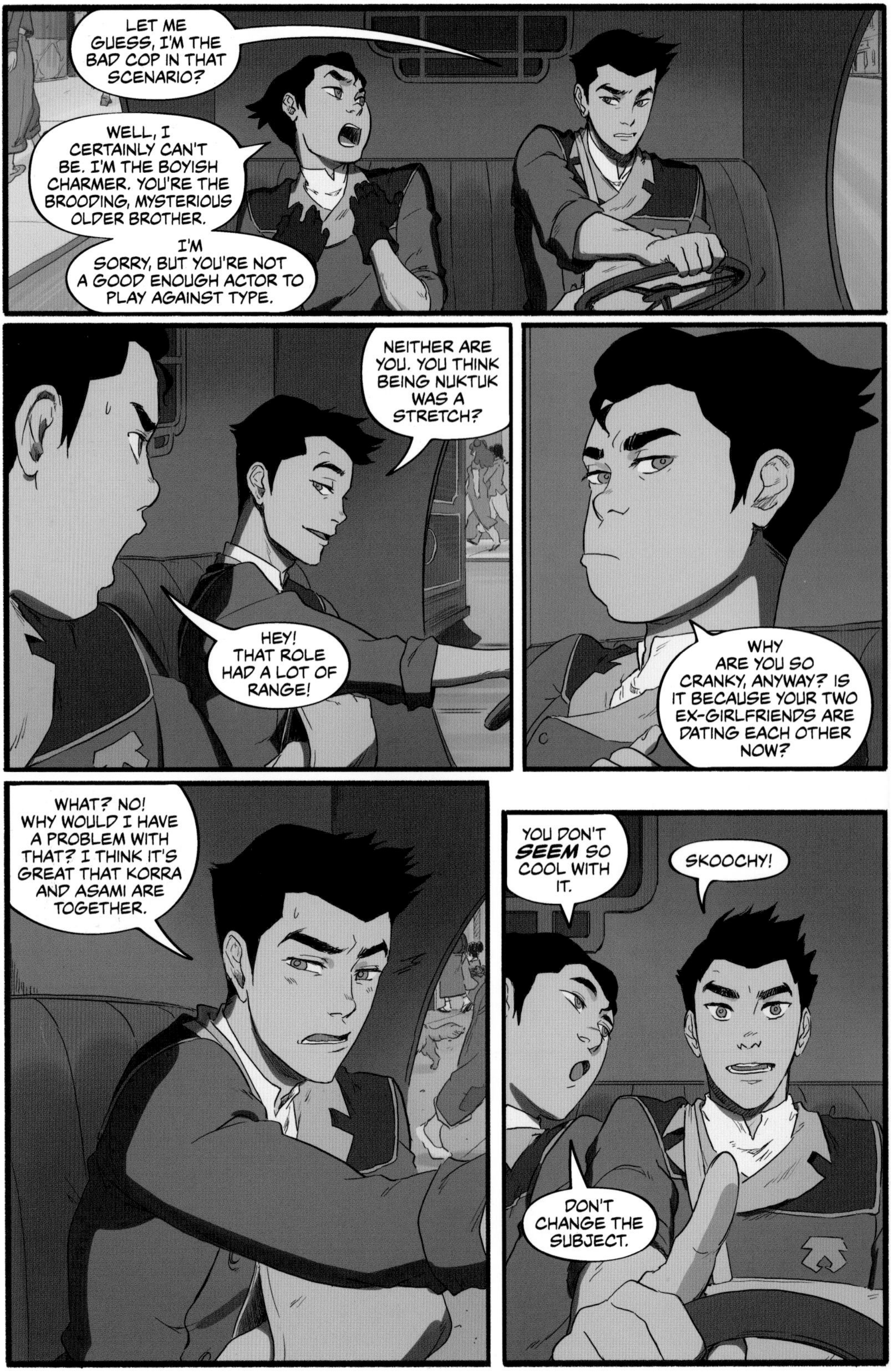
LET ME GUESS, I'M THE BAD COP IN THAT SCENARIO?
WELL, I CERTAINLY CAN'T BE. I'M THE BOYISH CHARMER. YOU'RE THE BROODING, MYSTERIOUS OLDER BROTHER.
I'M SORRY, BUT YOU'RE NOT A GOOD ENOUGH ACTOR TO PLAY AGAINST TYPE.
NEITHER ARE YOU. YOU THINK BEING NUKTUK WAS A STRETCH?
HEY! THAT ROLE HAD A LOT OF RANGE!
WHY ARE YOU SO CRANKY, ANYWAY? IS IT BECAUSE YOUR TWO EX-GIRLFRIENDS ARE DATING EACH OTHER NOW?
WHAT? NO! WHY WOULD I HAVE A PROBLEM WITH THAT? I THINK IT'S GREAT THAT KORRA AND ASAMI ARE TOGETHER.
YOU DON'T **SEEM** SO COOL WITH IT.
SKOOCHY!
DON'T CHANGE THE SUBJECT.

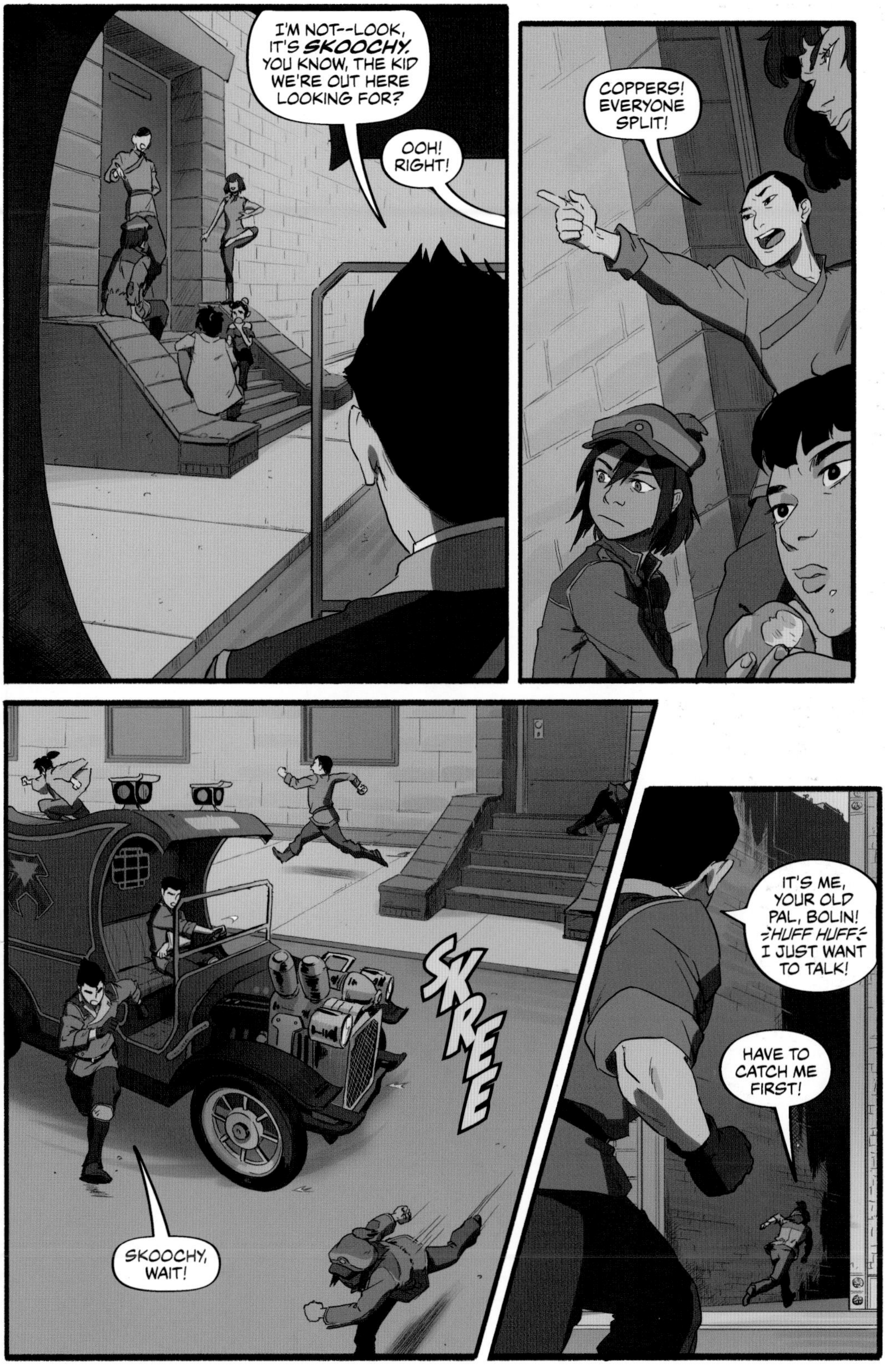
I'M NOT--LOOK, IT'S SKOOCHY. YOU KNOW, THE KID WE'RE OUT HERE LOOKING FOR?
OOH! RIGHT!
COPPERS! EVERYONE SPLIT!
SKREE
SKOOCHY, WAIT!
IT'S ME, YOUR OLD PAL, BOLIN! HUFF HUFF I JUST WANT TO TALK!
HAVE TO CATCH ME FIRST!

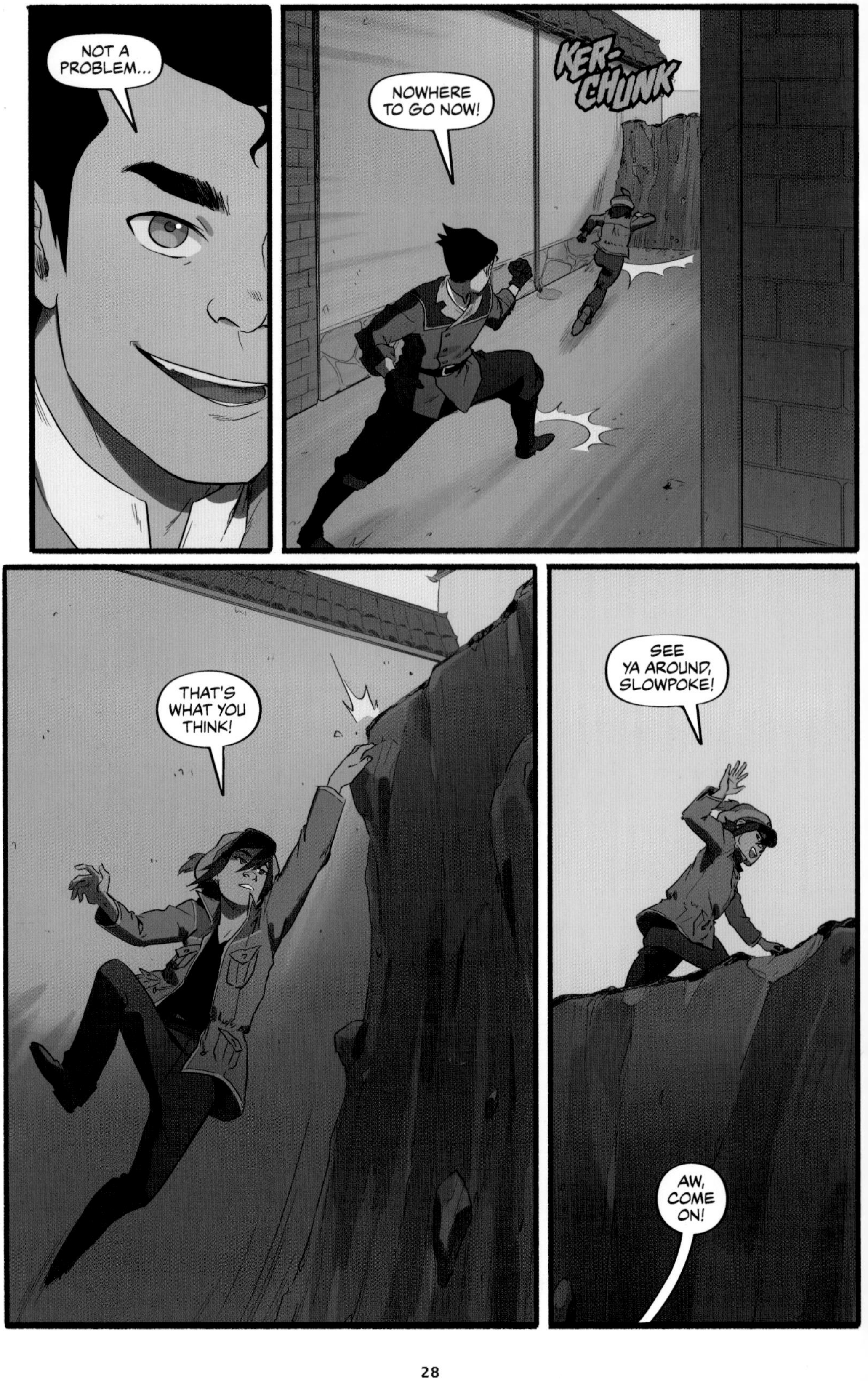
NOT A PROBLEM...
NOWHERE TO GO NOW!
KER-CHUNK
THAT'S WHAT YOU THINK!
SEE YA AROUND, SLOWPOKE!
AW, COME ON!

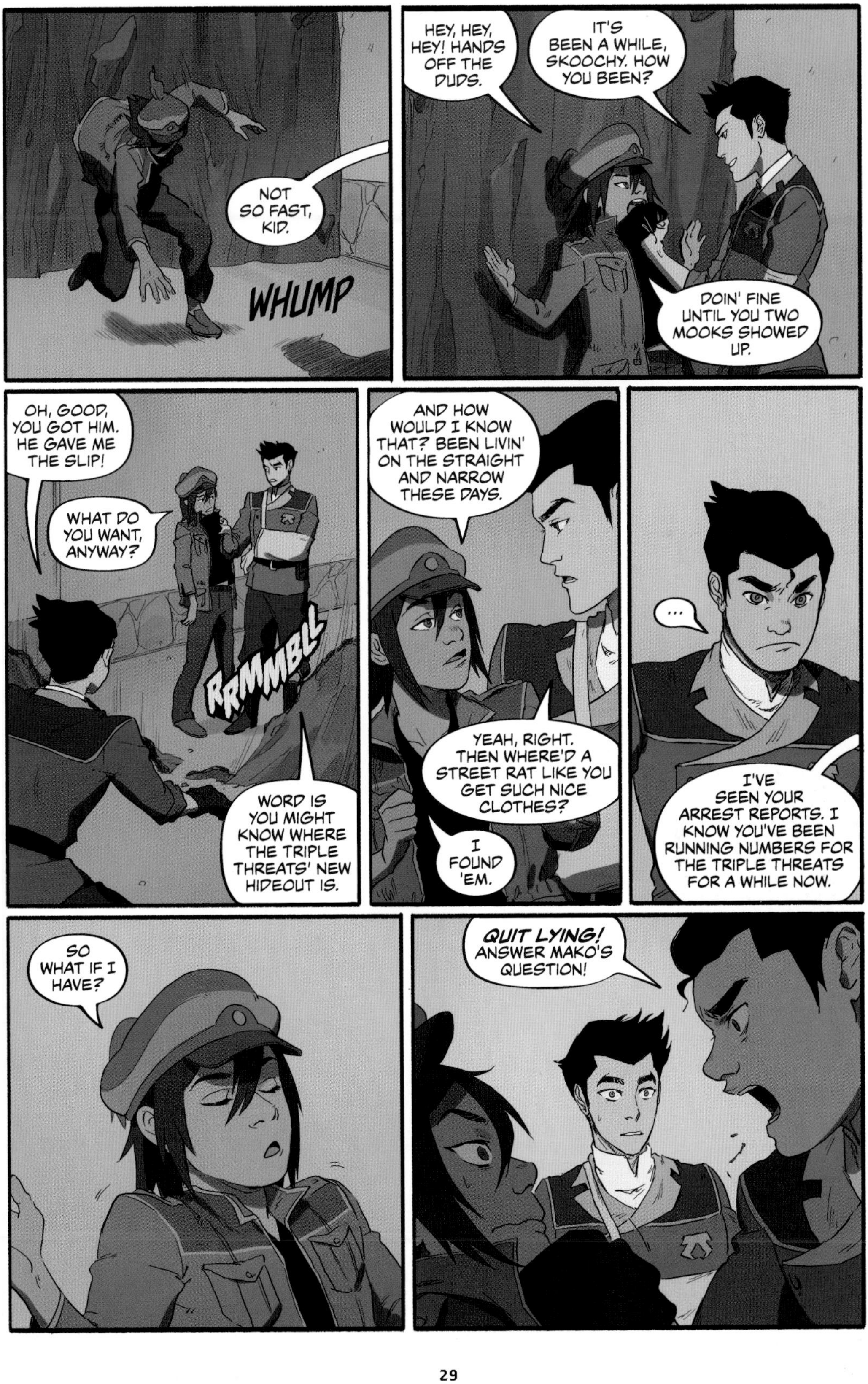
NOT SO FAST, KID.
WHUMP
HEY, HEY, HEY! HANDS OFF THE DUDS.
IT'S BEEN A WHILE, SKOOCHY. HOW YOU BEEN?
DOIN' FINE UNTIL YOU TWO MOOKS SHOWED UP.
OH, GOOD, YOU GOT HIM. HE GAVE ME THE SLIP!
WHAT DO YOU WANT, ANYWAY?
RRMMBLL
WORD IS YOU MIGHT KNOW WHERE THE TRIPLE THREATS' NEW HIDEOUT IS.
AND HOW WOULD I KNOW THAT? BEEN LIVIN' ON THE STRAIGHT AND NARROW THESE DAYS.
YEAH, RIGHT. THEN WHERE'D A STREET RAT LIKE YOU GET SUCH NICE CLOTHES?
I FOUND 'EM.
...
I'VE SEEN YOUR ARREST REPORTS. I KNOW YOU'VE BEEN RUNNING NUMBERS FOR THE TRIPLE THREATS FOR A WHILE NOW.
SO WHAT IF I HAVE?
QUIT LYING! ANSWER MAKO'S QUESTION!

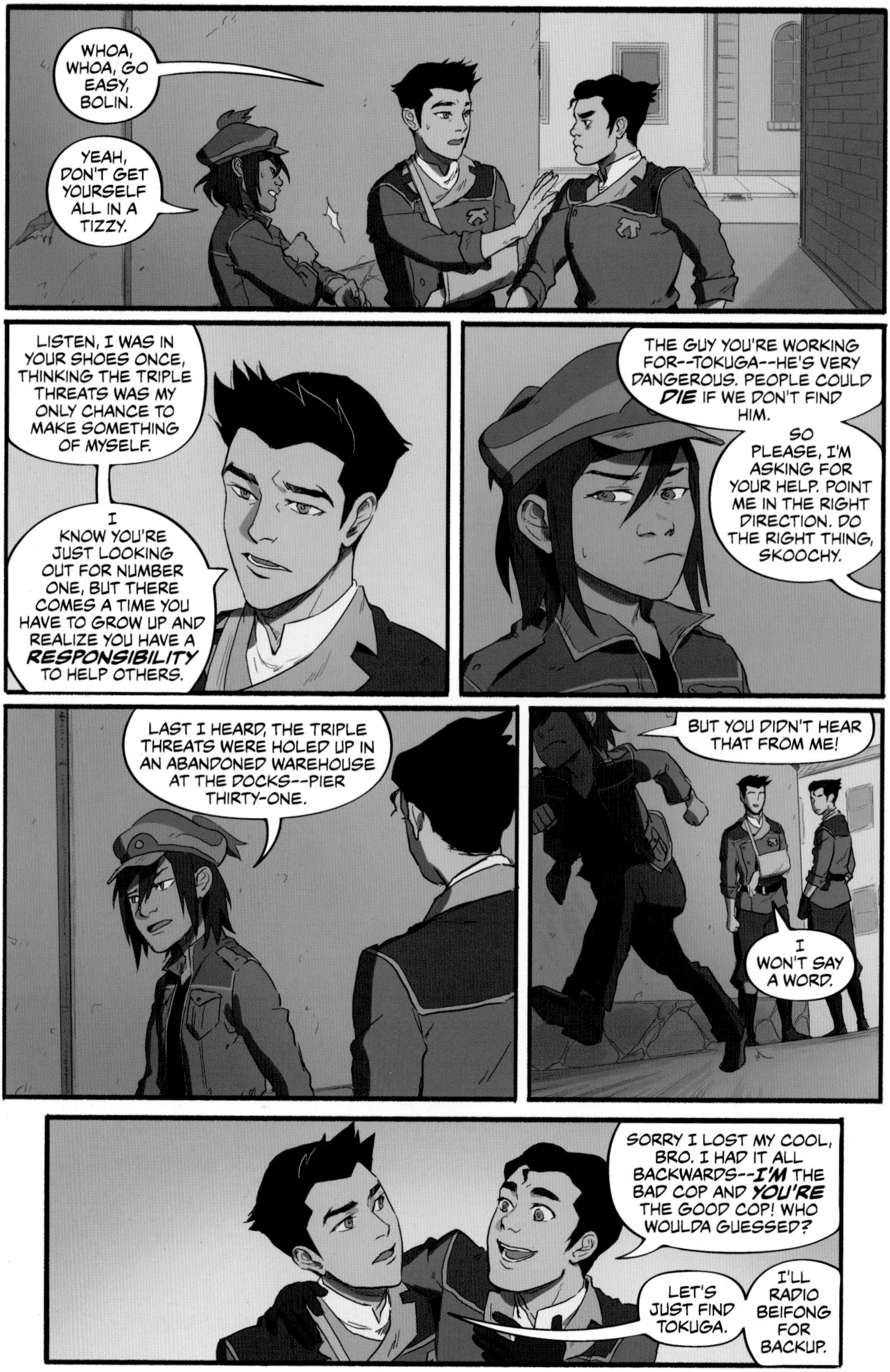
WHOA, WHOA, GO EASY, BOLIN.
YEAH, DON'T GET YOURSELF ALL IN A TIZZY.
LISTEN, I WAS IN YOUR SHOES ONCE, THINKING THE TRIPLE THREATS WAS MY ONLY CHANCE TO MAKE SOMETHING OF MYSELF.
I KNOW YOU'RE JUST LOOKING OUT FOR NUMBER ONE, BUT THERE COMES A TIME YOU HAVE TO GROW UP AND REALIZE YOU HAVE A RESPONSIBILITY TO HELP OTHERS.
THE GUY YOU'RE WORKING FOR--TOKUGA--HE'S VERY DANGEROUS. PEOPLE COULD DIE IF WE DON'T FIND HIM.
SO PLEASE, I'M ASKING FOR YOUR HELP. POINT ME IN THE RIGHT DIRECTION. DO THE RIGHT THING, SKOOCHY.
LAST I HEARD, THE TRIPLE THREATS WERE HOLED UP IN AN ABANDONED WAREHOUSE AT THE DOCKS--PIER THIRTY-ONE.
BUT YOU DIDN'T HEAR THAT FROM ME!
I WON'T SAY A WORD.
SORRY I LOST MY COOL, BRO. I HAD IT ALL BACKWARDS--I'M THE BAD COP AND YOU'RE THE GOOD COP! WHO WOULDA GUESSED?
LET'S JUST FIND TOKUGA.
I'LL RADIO BEIFONG FOR BACKUP.

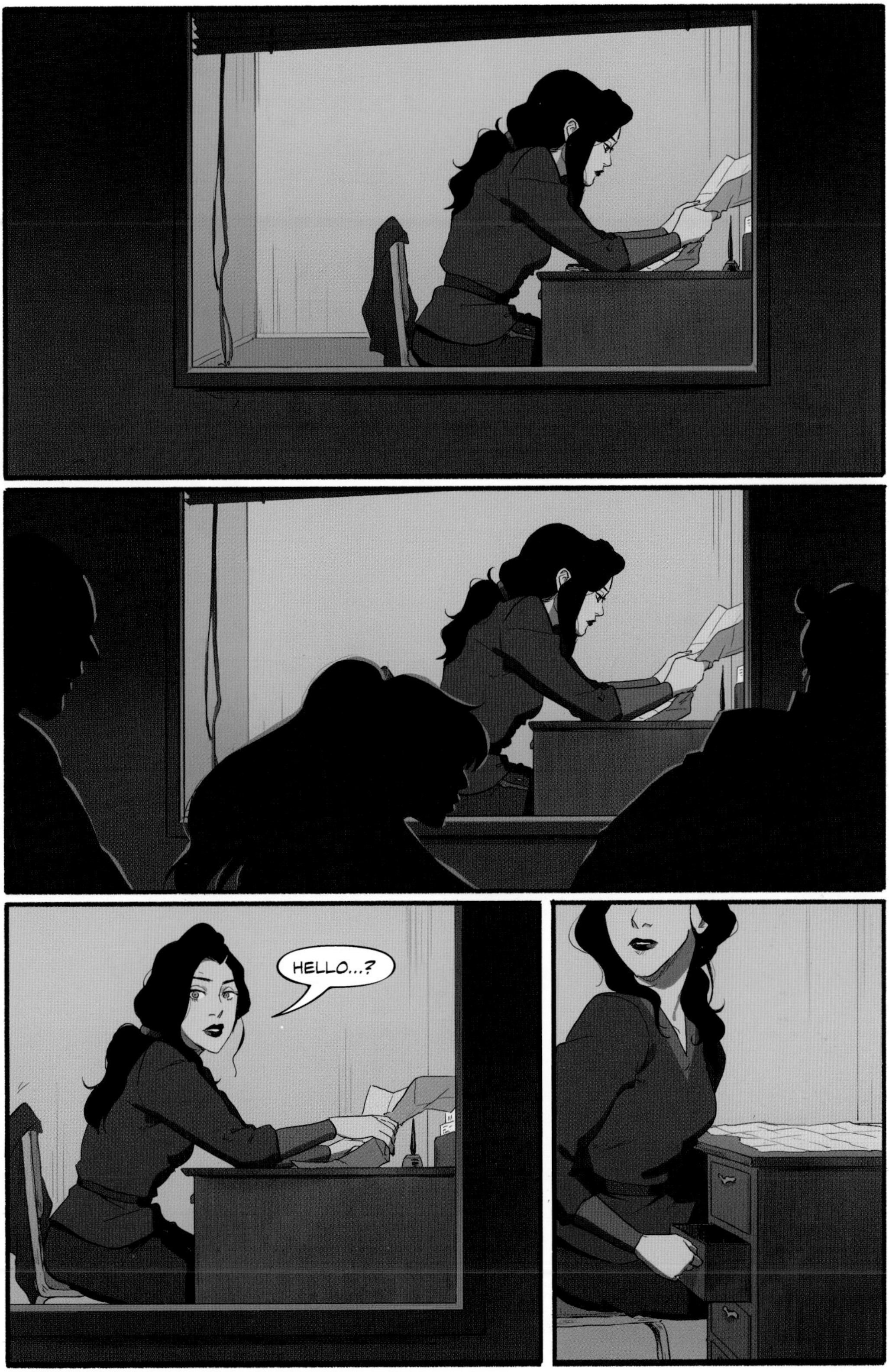
HELLO...?

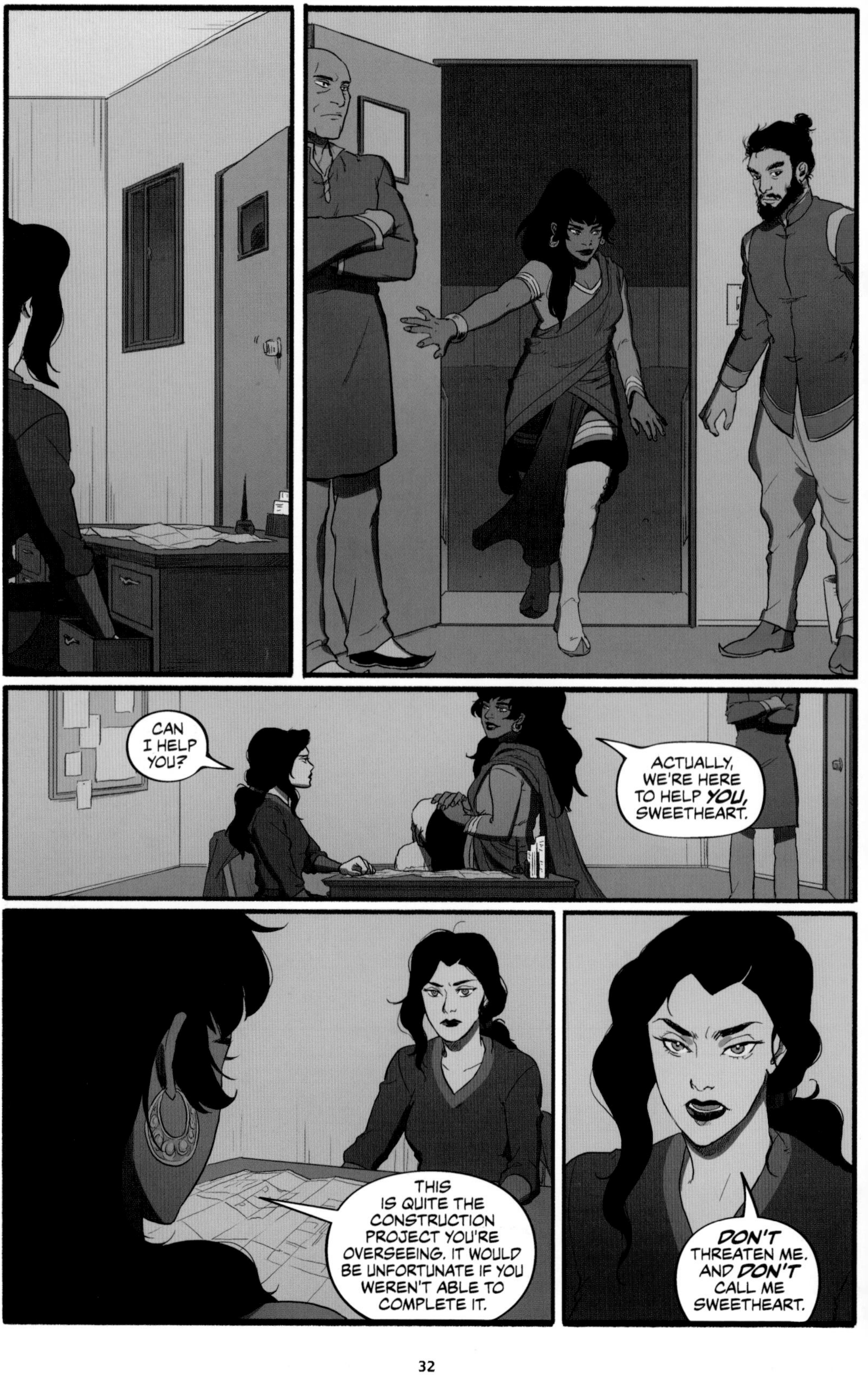
CAN I HELP YOU?
ACTUALLY, WE'RE HERE TO HELP YOU, SWEETHEART.
THIS IS QUITE THE CONSTRUCTION PROJECT YOU'RE OVERSEEING. IT WOULD BE UNFORTUNATE IF YOU WEREN'T ABLE TO COMPLETE IT.
DON'T THREATEN ME. AND DON'T CALL ME SWEETHEART.

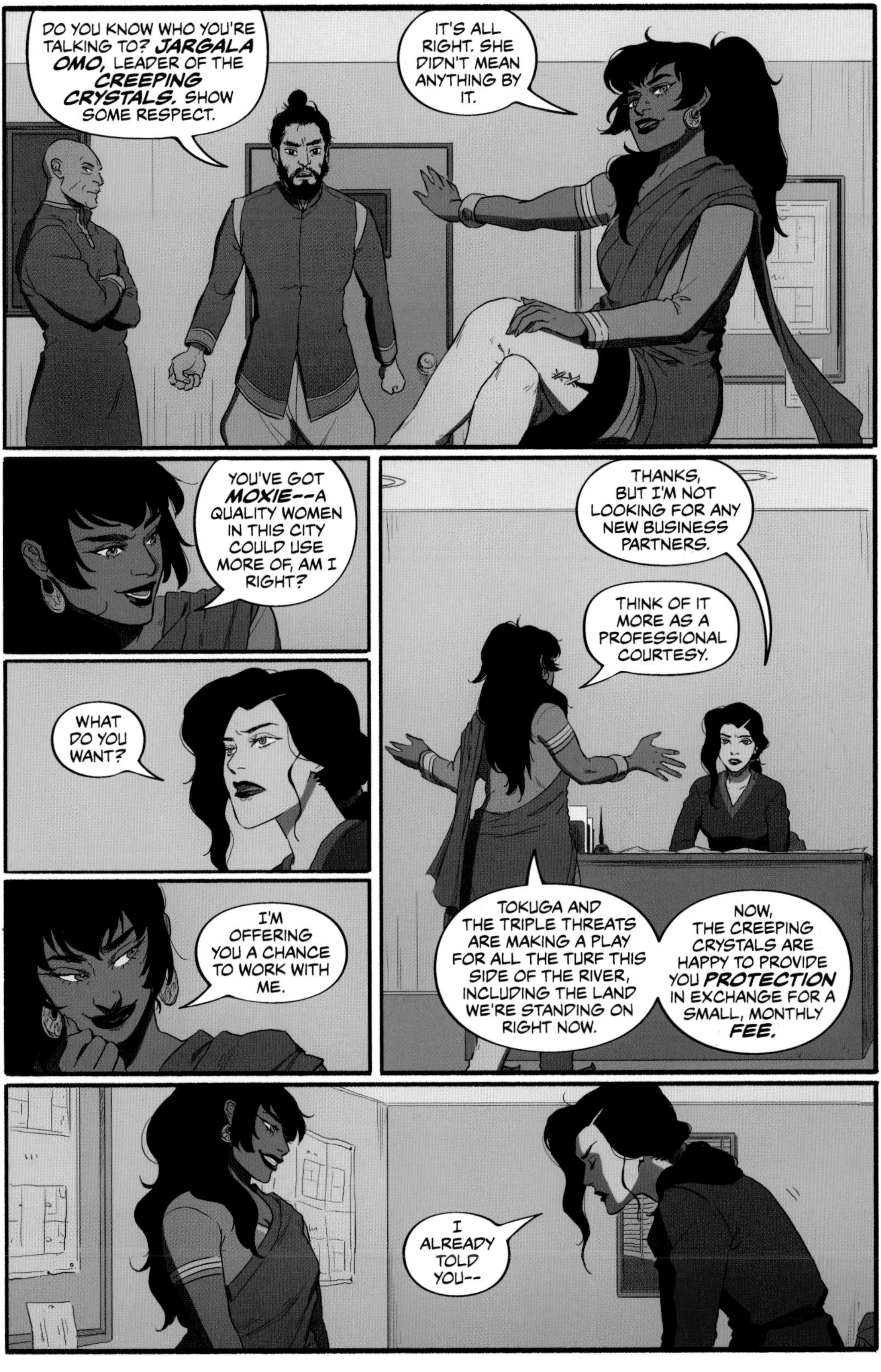
DO YOU KNOW WHO YOU'RE TALKING TO? JARGALA OMO, LEADER OF THE CREEPING CRYSTALS. SHOW SOME RESPECT.
IT'S ALL RIGHT. SHE DIDN'T MEAN ANYTHING BY IT.
YOU'VE GOT MOXIE--A QUALITY WOMEN IN THIS CITY COULD USE MORE OF, AM I RIGHT?
WHAT DO YOU WANT?
I'M OFFERING YOU A CHANCE TO WORK WITH ME.
THANKS, BUT I'M NOT LOOKING FOR ANY NEW BUSINESS PARTNERS.
THINK OF IT MORE AS A PROFESSIONAL COURTESY.
TOKUGA AND THE TRIPLE THREATS ARE MAKING A PLAY FOR ALL THE TURF THIS SIDE OF THE RIVER, INCLUDING THE LAND WE'RE STANDING ON RIGHT NOW.
NOW, THE CREEPING CRYSTALS ARE HAPPY TO PROVIDE YOU PROTECTION IN EXCHANGE FOR A SMALL, MONTHLY FEE.
I ALREADY TOLD YOU--

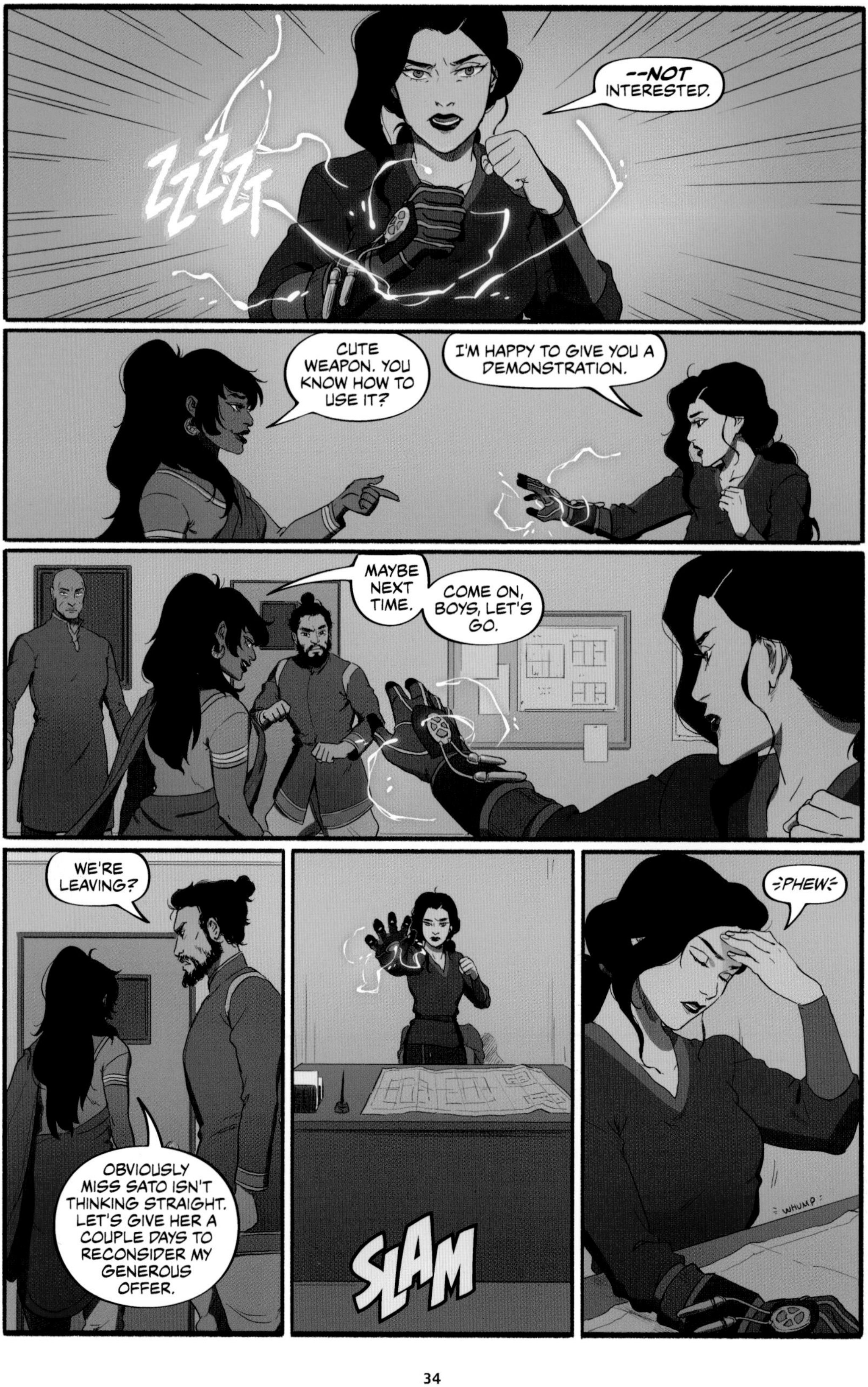
--NOT INTERESTED.
ZZZZT
CUTE WEAPON. YOU KNOW HOW TO USE IT?
I'M HAPPY TO GIVE YOU A DEMONSTRATION.
MAYBE NEXT TIME.
COME ON, BOYS, LET'S GO.
WE'RE LEAVING?
OBVIOUSLY MISS SATO ISN'T THINKING STRAIGHT. LET'S GIVE HER A COUPLE DAYS TO RECONSIDER MY GENEROUS OFFER.
SLAM
PHEW
WHUMP

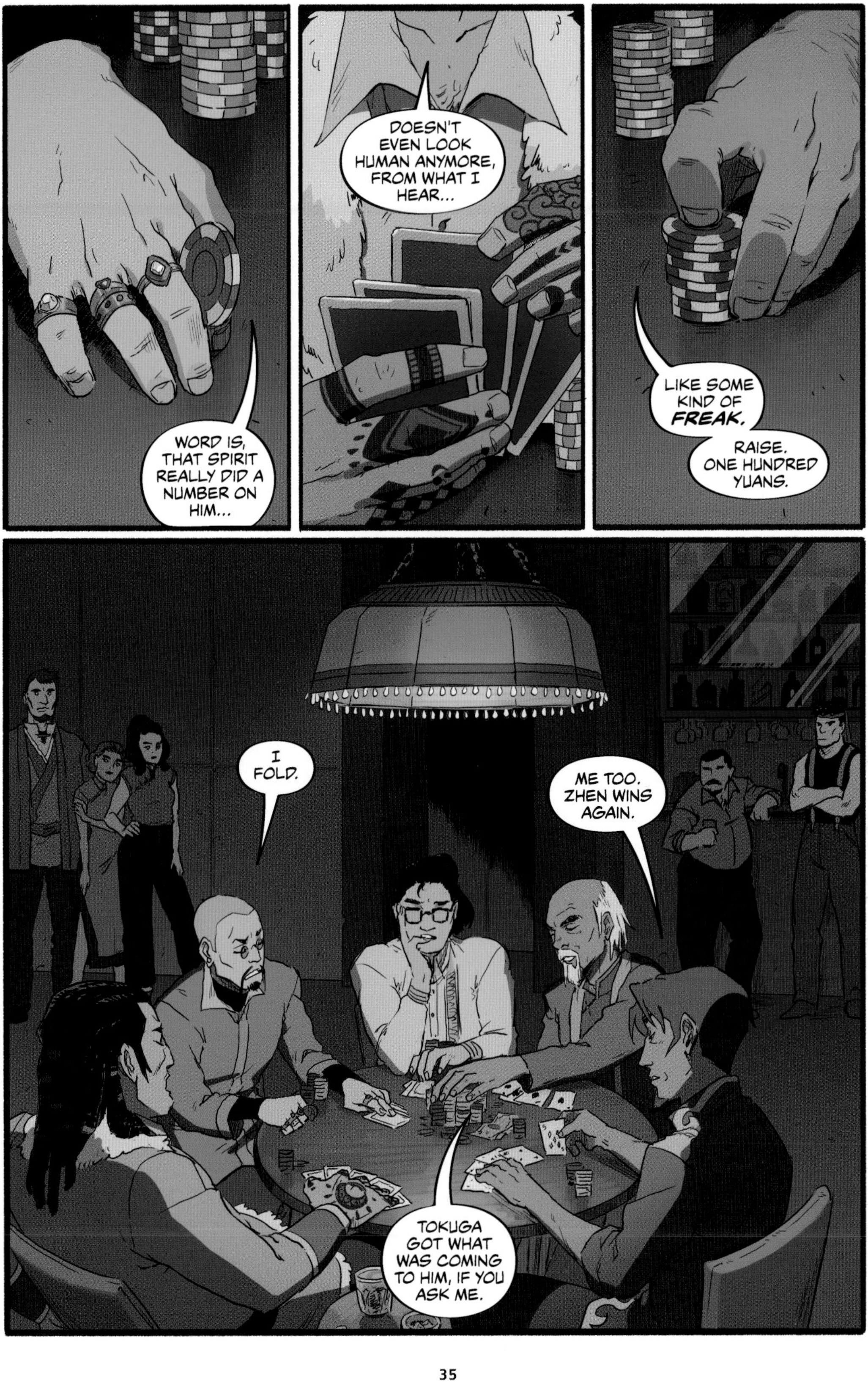
WORD IS, THAT SPIRIT REALLY DID A NUMBER ON HIM...
DOESN'T EVEN LOOK HUMAN ANYMORE, FROM WHAT I HEAR...
LIKE SOME KIND OF **FREAK.**
RAISE. ONE HUNDRED YUANS.
I FOLD.
ME TOO. ZHEN WINS AGAIN.
TOKUGA GOT WHAT WAS COMING TO HIM, IF YOU ASK ME.

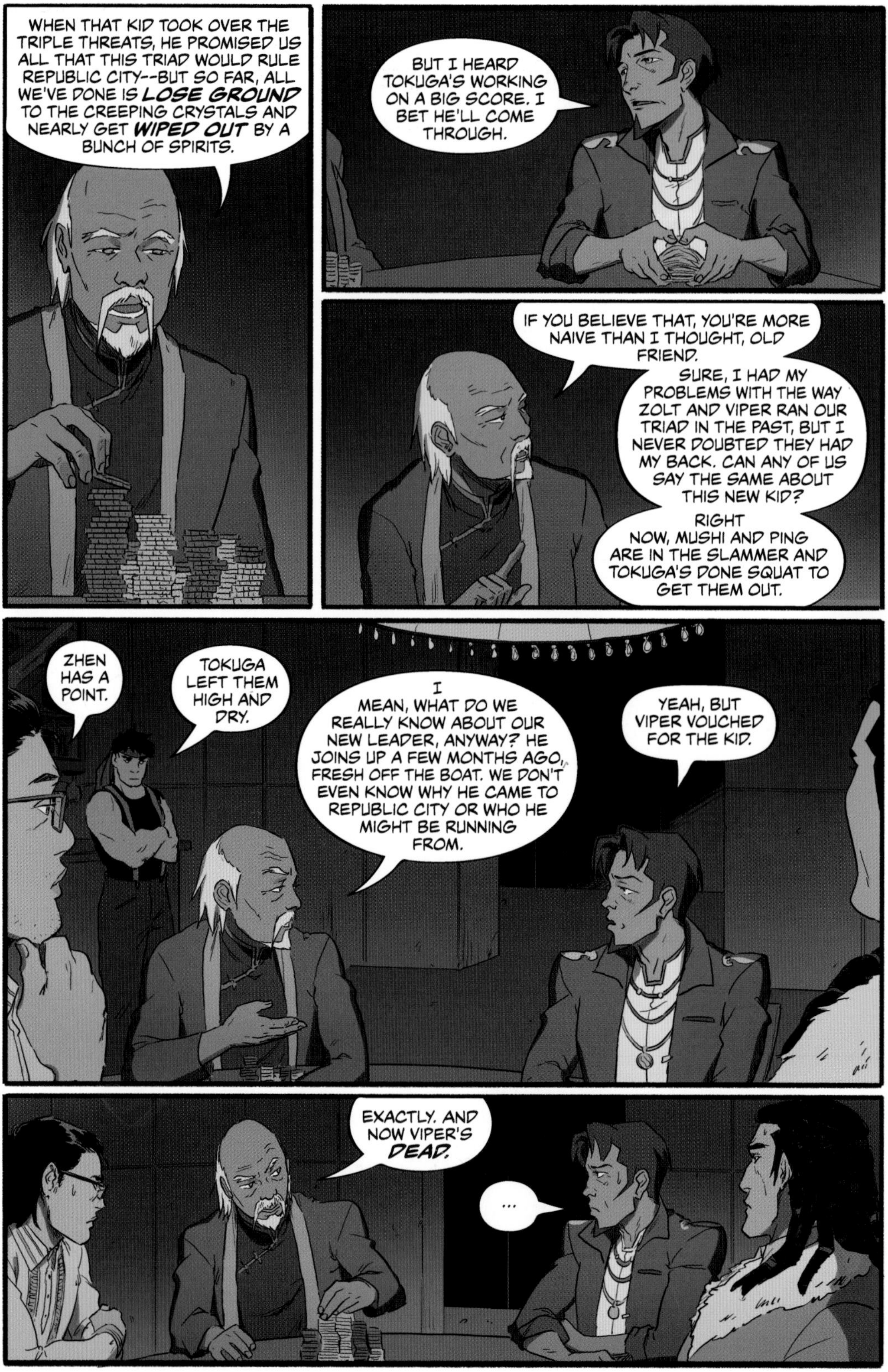
WHEN THAT KID TOOK OVER THE TRIPLE THREATS, HE PROMISED US ALL THAT THIS TRIAD WOULD RULE REPUBLIC CITY--BUT SO FAR, ALL WE'VE DONE IS LOSE GROUND TO THE CREEPING CRYSTALS AND NEARLY GET WIPED OUT BY A BUNCH OF SPIRITS.
BUT I HEARD TOKUGA'S WORKING ON A BIG SCORE. I BET HE'LL COME THROUGH.
IF YOU BELIEVE THAT, YOU'RE MORE NAIVE THAN I THOUGHT, OLD FRIEND.
SURE, I HAD MY PROBLEMS WITH THE WAY ZOLT AND VIPER RAN OUR TRIAD IN THE PAST, BUT I NEVER DOUBTED THEY HAD MY BACK. CAN ANY OF US SAY THE SAME ABOUT THIS NEW KID?
RIGHT NOW, MUSHI AND PING ARE IN THE SLAMMER AND TOKUGA'S DONE SQUAT TO GET THEM OUT.
ZHEN HAS A POINT.
TOKUGA LEFT THEM HIGH AND DRY.
I MEAN, WHAT DO WE REALLY KNOW ABOUT OUR NEW LEADER, ANYWAY? HE JOINS UP A FEW MONTHS AGO, FRESH OFF THE BOAT. WE DON'T EVEN KNOW WHY HE CAME TO REPUBLIC CITY OR WHO HE MIGHT BE RUNNING FROM.
YEAH, BUT VIPER VOUCHED FOR THE KID.
EXACTLY. AND NOW VIPER'S DEAD.
...

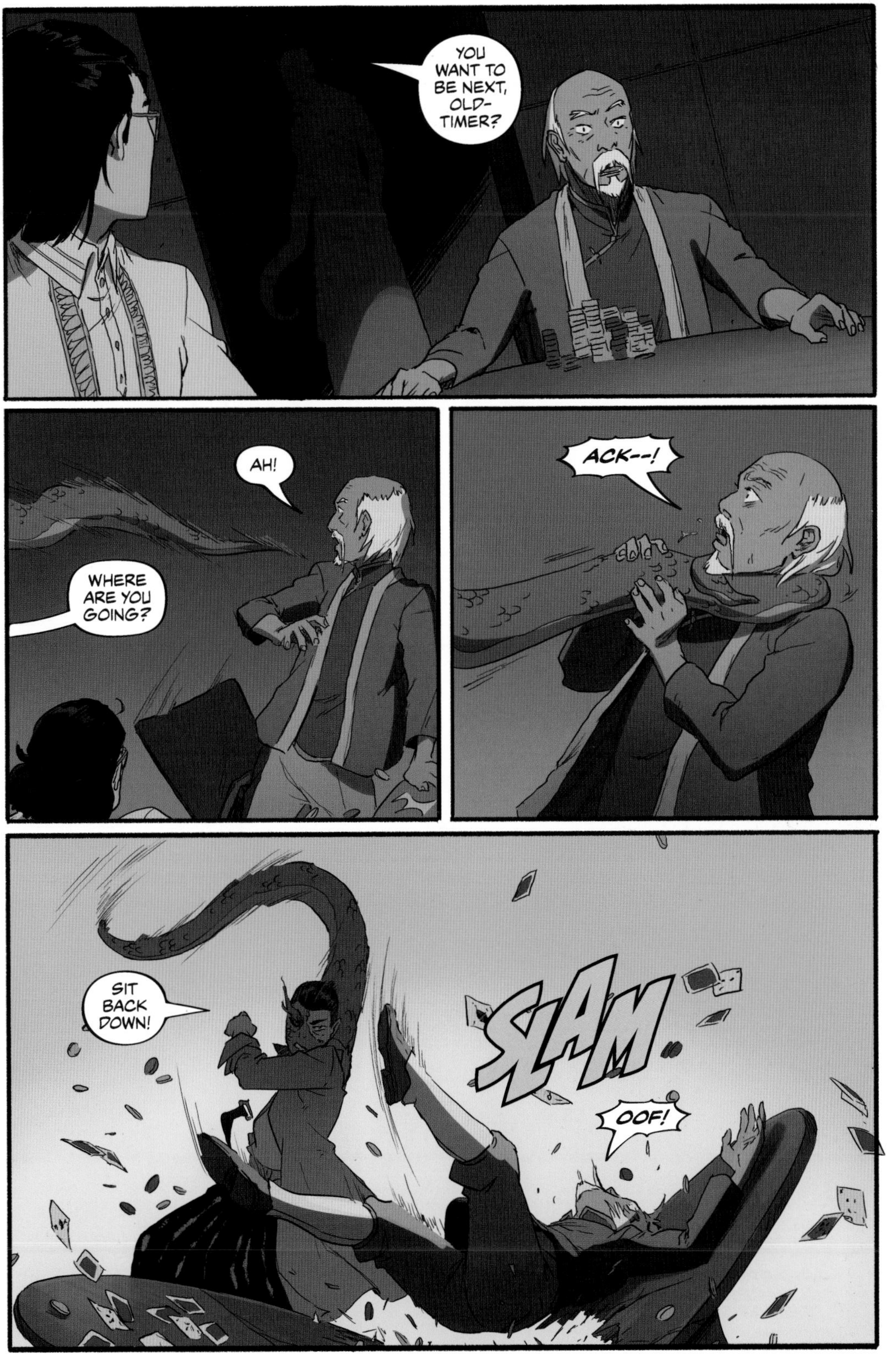
YOU WANT TO BE NEXT, OLD-TIMER?
AH!
WHERE ARE YOU GOING?
ACK--!
SIT BACK DOWN!
SLAM
OOF!

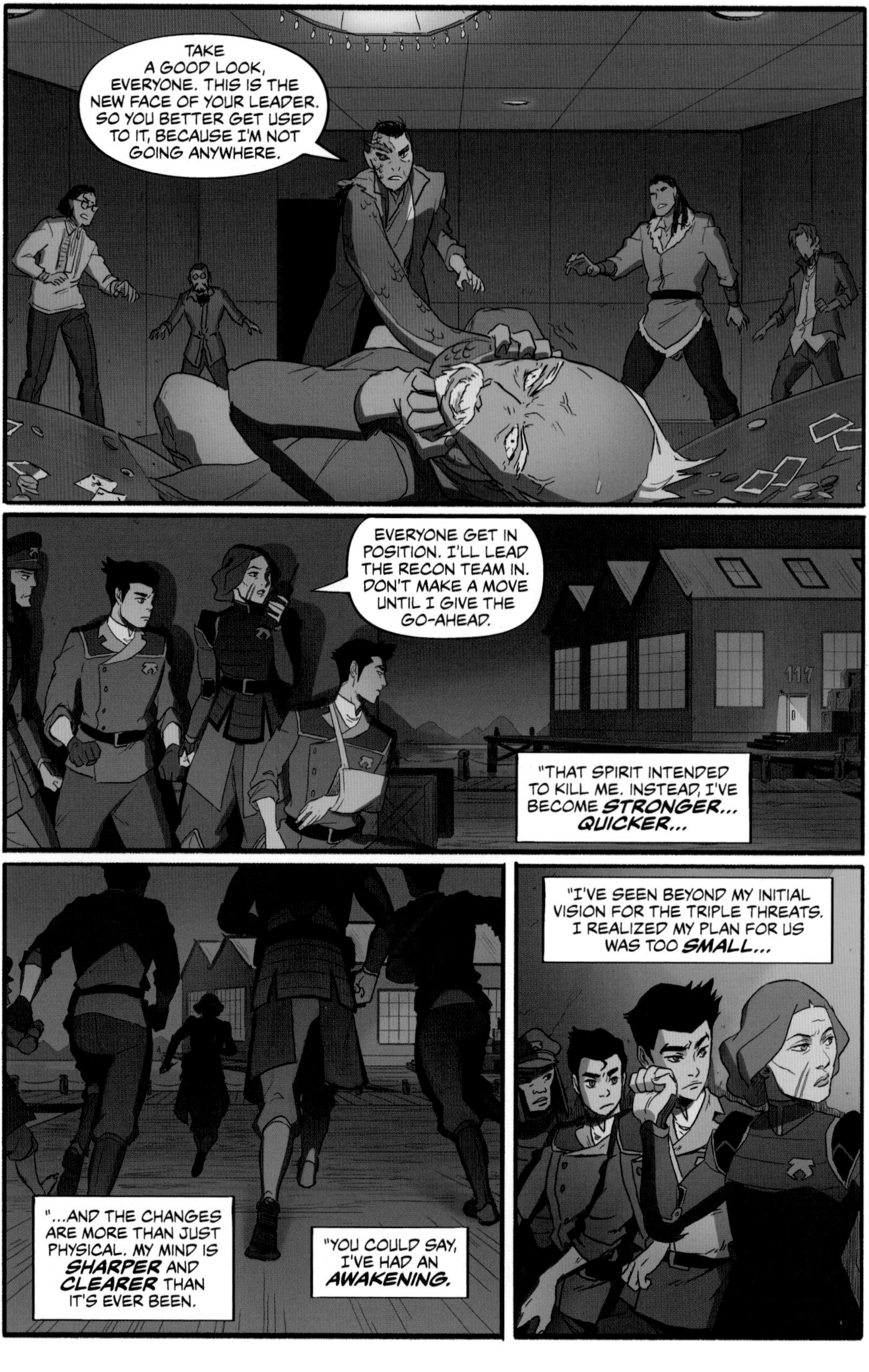
TAKE A GOOD LOOK, EVERYONE. THIS IS THE NEW FACE OF YOUR LEADER. SO YOU BETTER GET USED TO IT, BECAUSE I'M NOT GOING ANYWHERE.
EVERYONE GET IN POSITION. I'LL LEAD THE RECON TEAM IN. DON'T MAKE A MOVE UNTIL I GIVE THE GO-AHEAD.
117
"THAT SPIRIT INTENDED TO KILL ME. INSTEAD, I'VE BECOME ***STRONGER... QUICKER...***
"...AND THE CHANGES ARE MORE THAN JUST PHYSICAL. MY MIND IS ***SHARPER*** AND ***CLEARER*** THAN IT'S EVER BEEN.
"YOU COULD SAY, I'VE HAD AN ***AWAKENING.***
"I'VE SEEN BEYOND MY INITIAL VISION FOR THE TRIPLE THREATS. I REALIZED MY PLAN FOR US WAS TOO ***SMALL...***

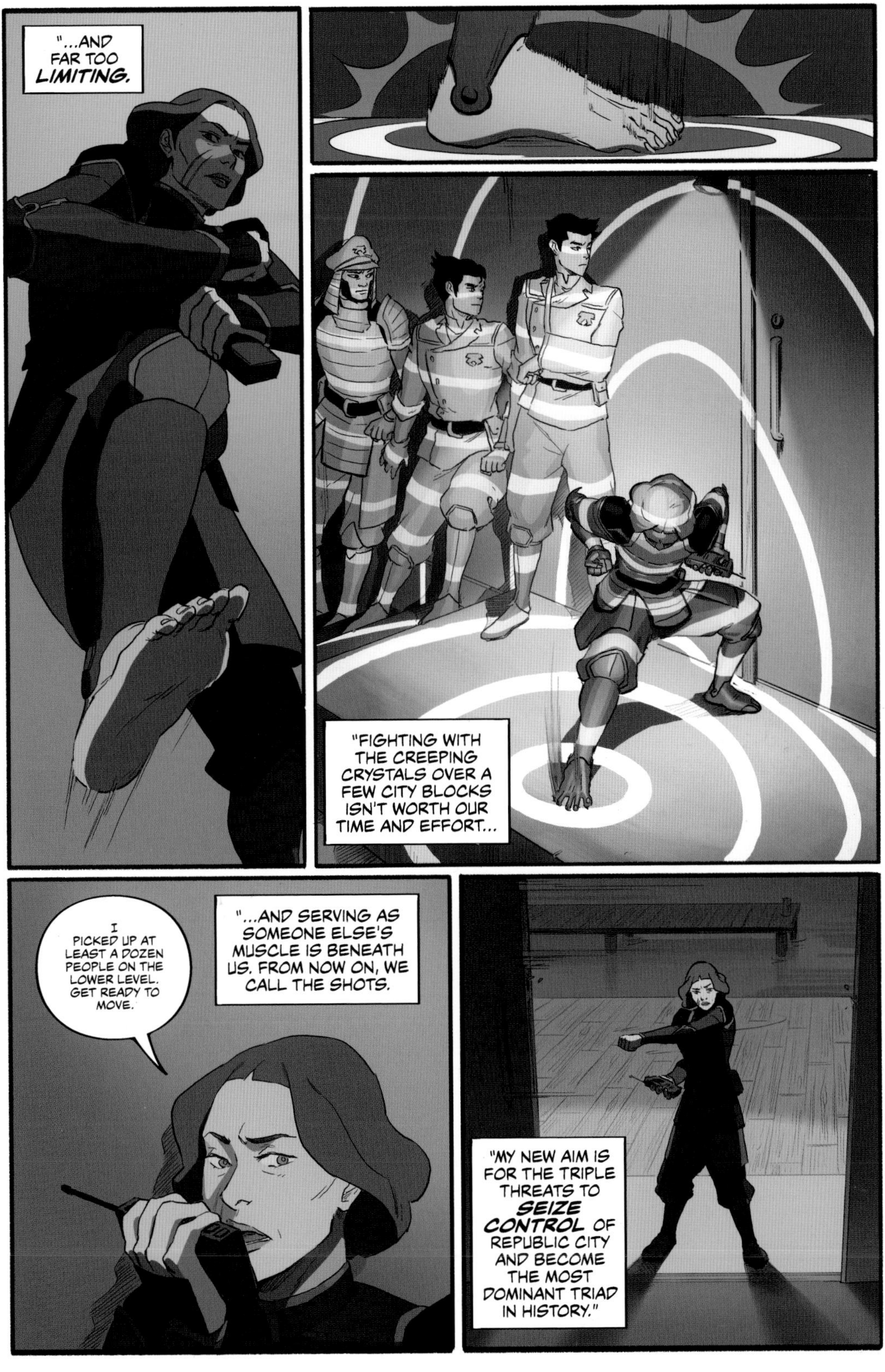
"...AND FAR TOO LIMITING.
"FIGHTING WITH THE CREEPING CRYSTALS OVER A FEW CITY BLOCKS ISN'T WORTH OUR TIME AND EFFORT...
I PICKED UP AT LEAST A DOZEN PEOPLE ON THE LOWER LEVEL. GET READY TO MOVE.
"...AND SERVING AS SOMEONE ELSE'S MUSCLE IS BENEATH US. FROM NOW ON, WE CALL THE SHOTS.
"MY NEW AIM IS FOR THE TRIPLE THREATS TO SEIZE CONTROL OF REPUBLIC CITY AND BECOME THE MOST DOMINANT TRIAD IN HISTORY."

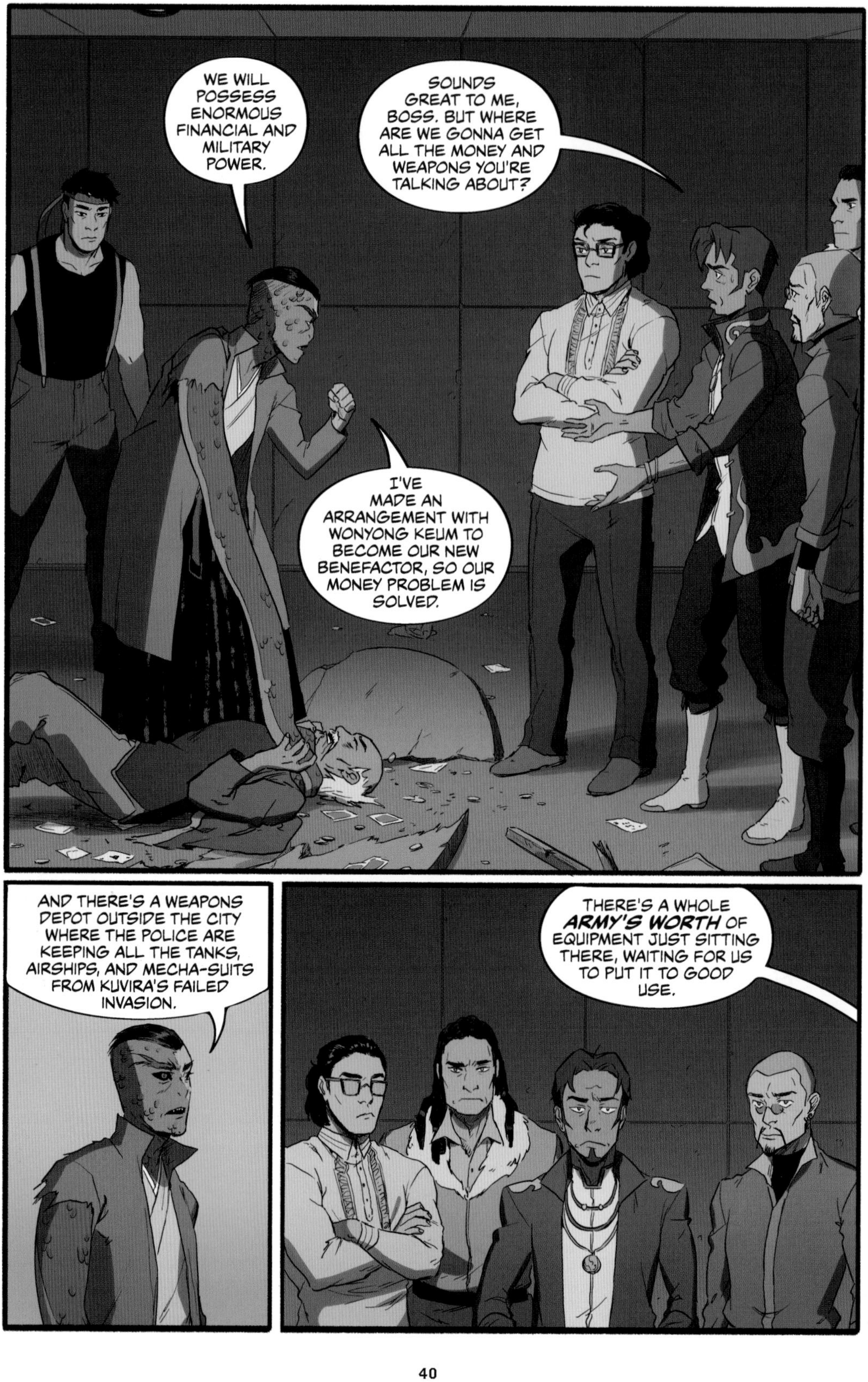
WE WILL POSSESS ENORMOUS FINANCIAL AND MILITARY POWER.
SOUNDS GREAT TO ME, BOSS. BUT WHERE ARE WE GONNA GET ALL THE MONEY AND WEAPONS YOU'RE TALKING ABOUT?
I'VE MADE AN ARRANGEMENT WITH WONYONG KEUM TO BECOME OUR NEW BENEFACTOR, SO OUR MONEY PROBLEM IS SOLVED.
AND THERE'S A WEAPONS DEPOT OUTSIDE THE CITY WHERE THE POLICE ARE KEEPING ALL THE TANKS, AIRSHIPS, AND MECHA-SUITS FROM KUVIRA'S FAILED INVASION.
THERE'S A WHOLE ***ARMY'S WORTH*** OF EQUIPMENT JUST SITTING THERE, WAITING FOR US TO PUT IT TO GOOD USE.

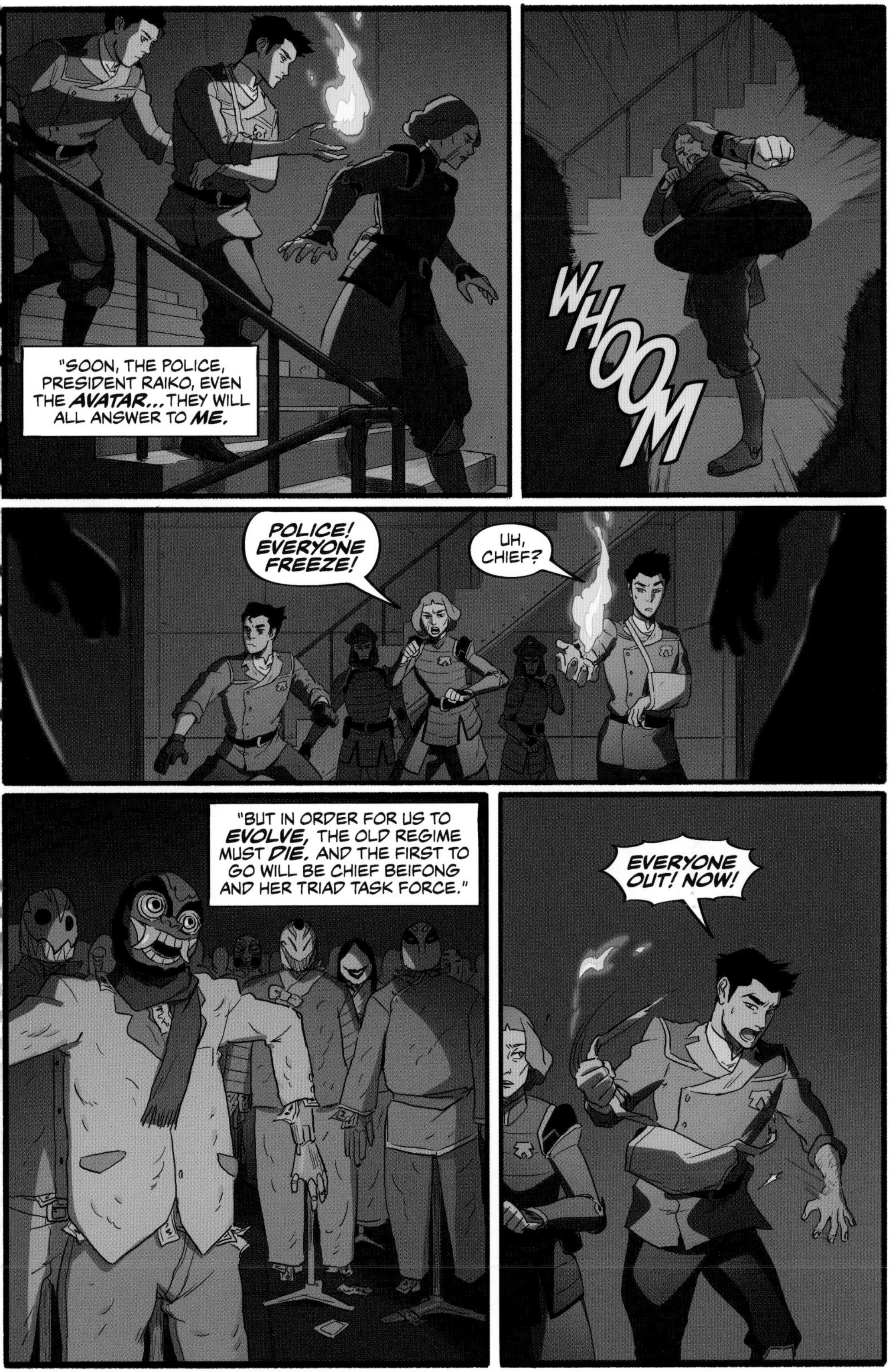
"SOON, THE POLICE, PRESIDENT RAIKO, EVEN THE AVATAR... THEY WILL ALL ANSWER TO ME.
WHOOM
POLICE! EVERYONE FREEZE!
UH, CHIEF?
"BUT IN ORDER FOR US TO EVOLVE, THE OLD REGIME MUST DIE. AND THE FIRST TO GO WILL BE CHIEF BEIFONG AND HER TRIAD TASK FORCE."
EVERYONE OUT! NOW!

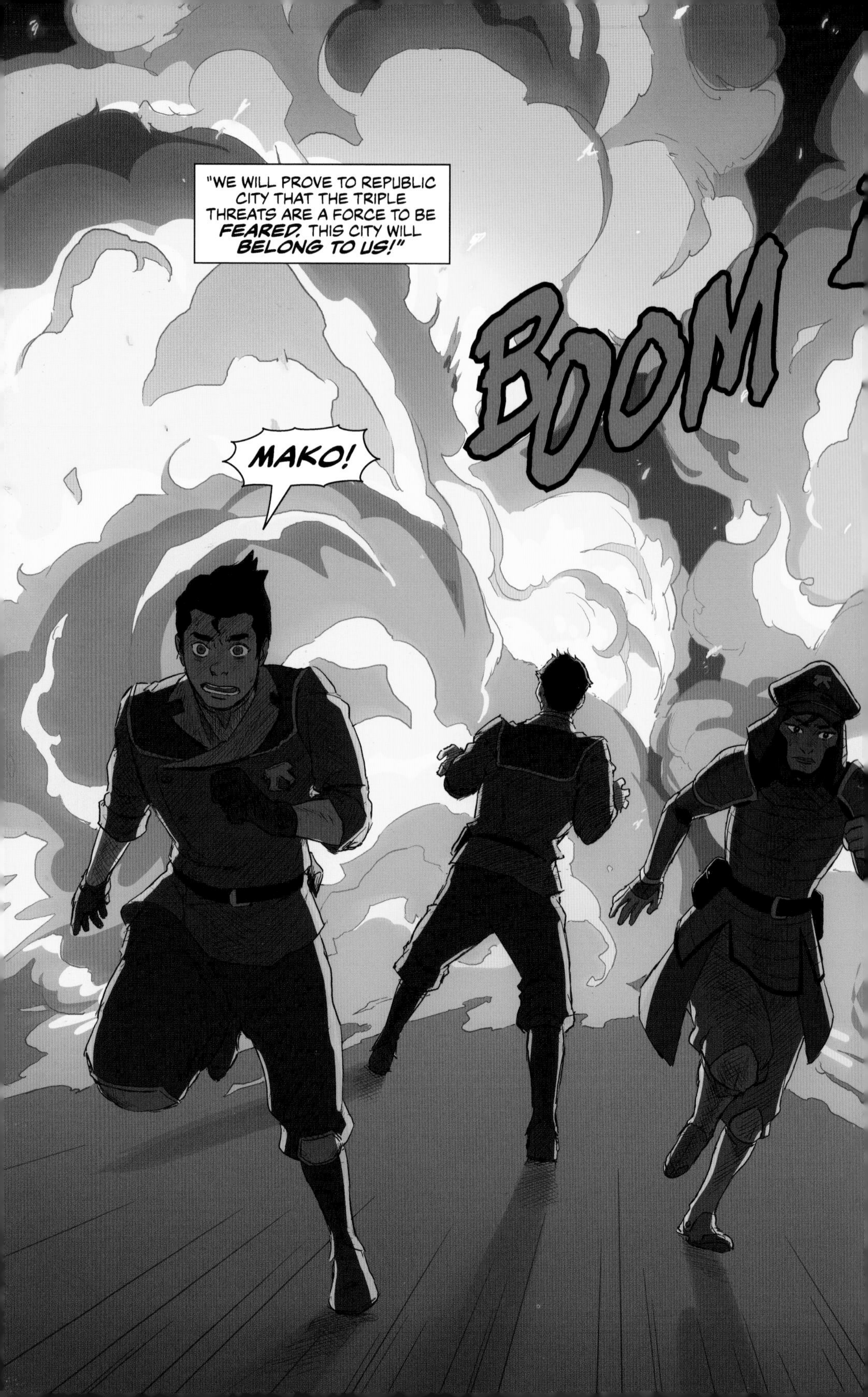
"WE WILL PROVE TO REPUBLIC CITY THAT THE TRIPLE THREATS ARE A FORCE TO BE FEARED. THIS CITY WILL BELONG TO US!"
BOOM
MAKO!

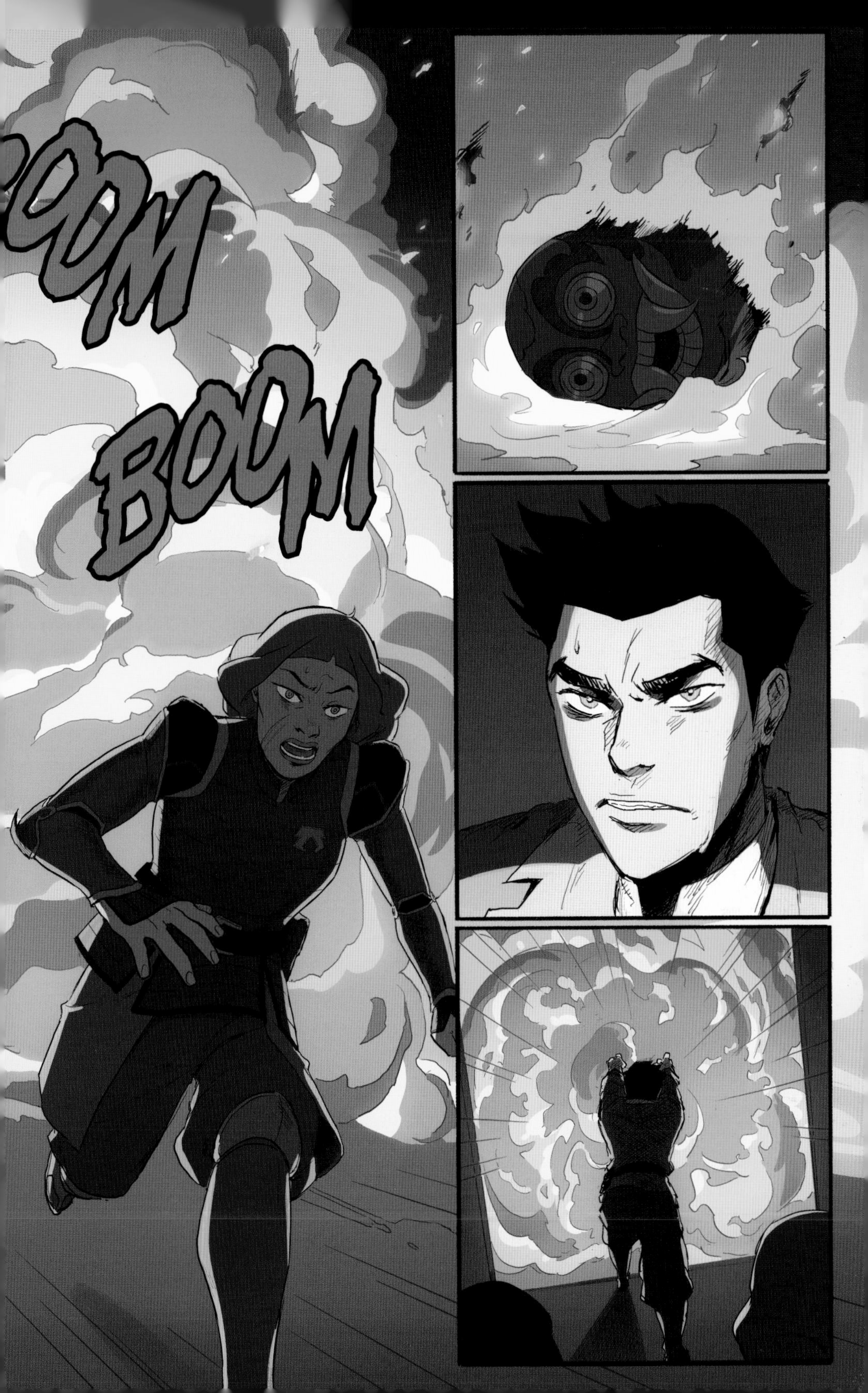
BOOM
BOOM

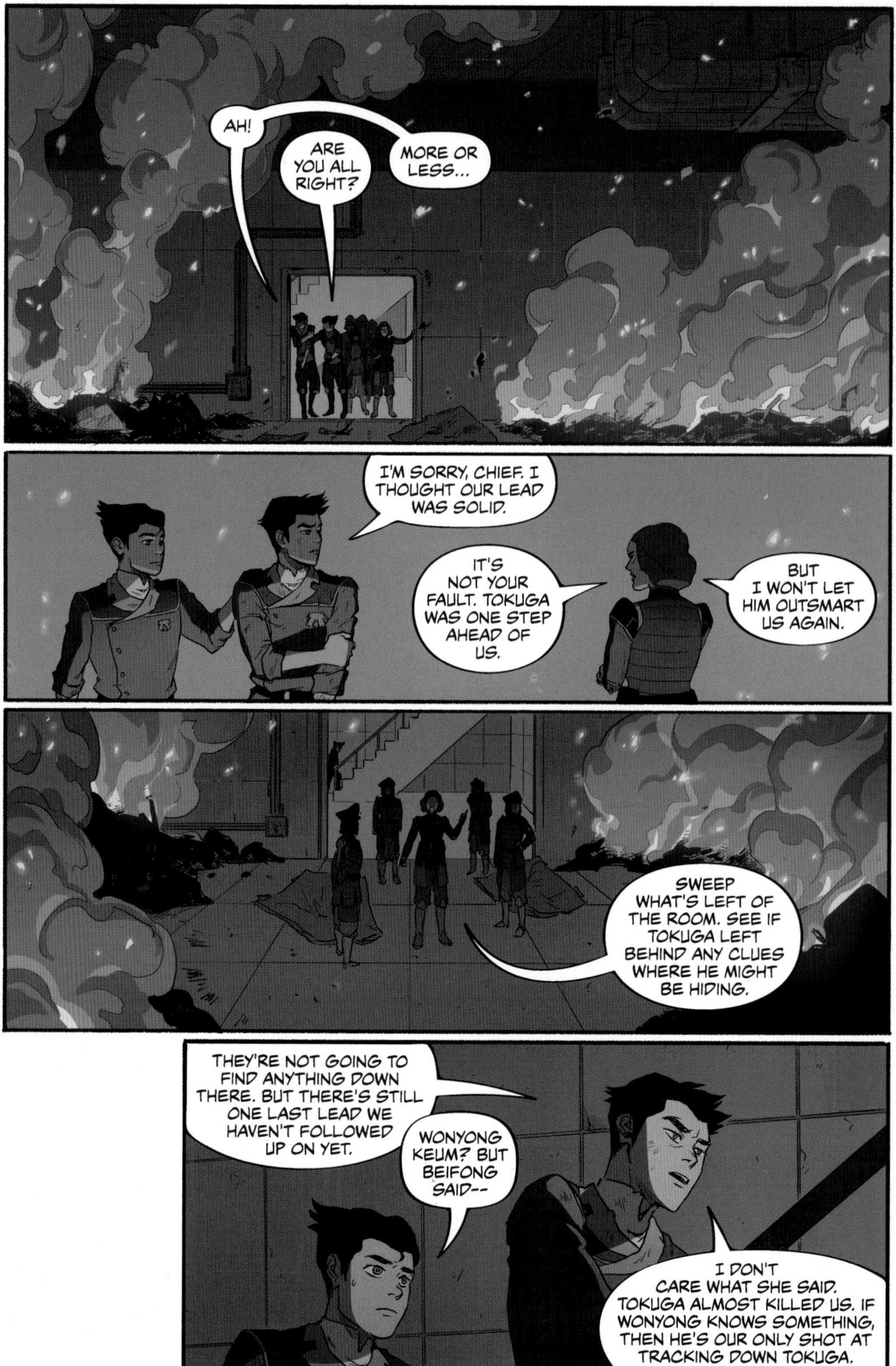
AH!
ARE YOU ALL RIGHT?
MORE OR LESS...
I'M SORRY, CHIEF. I THOUGHT OUR LEAD WAS SOLID.
IT'S NOT YOUR FAULT. TOKUGA WAS ONE STEP AHEAD OF US.
BUT I WON'T LET HIM OUTSMART US AGAIN.
SWEEP WHAT'S LEFT OF THE ROOM. SEE IF TOKUGA LEFT BEHIND ANY CLUES WHERE HE MIGHT BE HIDING.
THEY'RE NOT GOING TO FIND ANYTHING DOWN THERE. BUT THERE'S STILL ONE LAST LEAD WE HAVEN'T FOLLOWED UP ON YET.
WONYONG KEUM? BUT BEIFONG SAID--
I DON'T CARE WHAT SHE SAID. TOKUGA ALMOST KILLED US. IF WONYONG KNOWS SOMETHING, THEN HE'S OUR ONLY SHOT AT TRACKING DOWN TOKUGA.

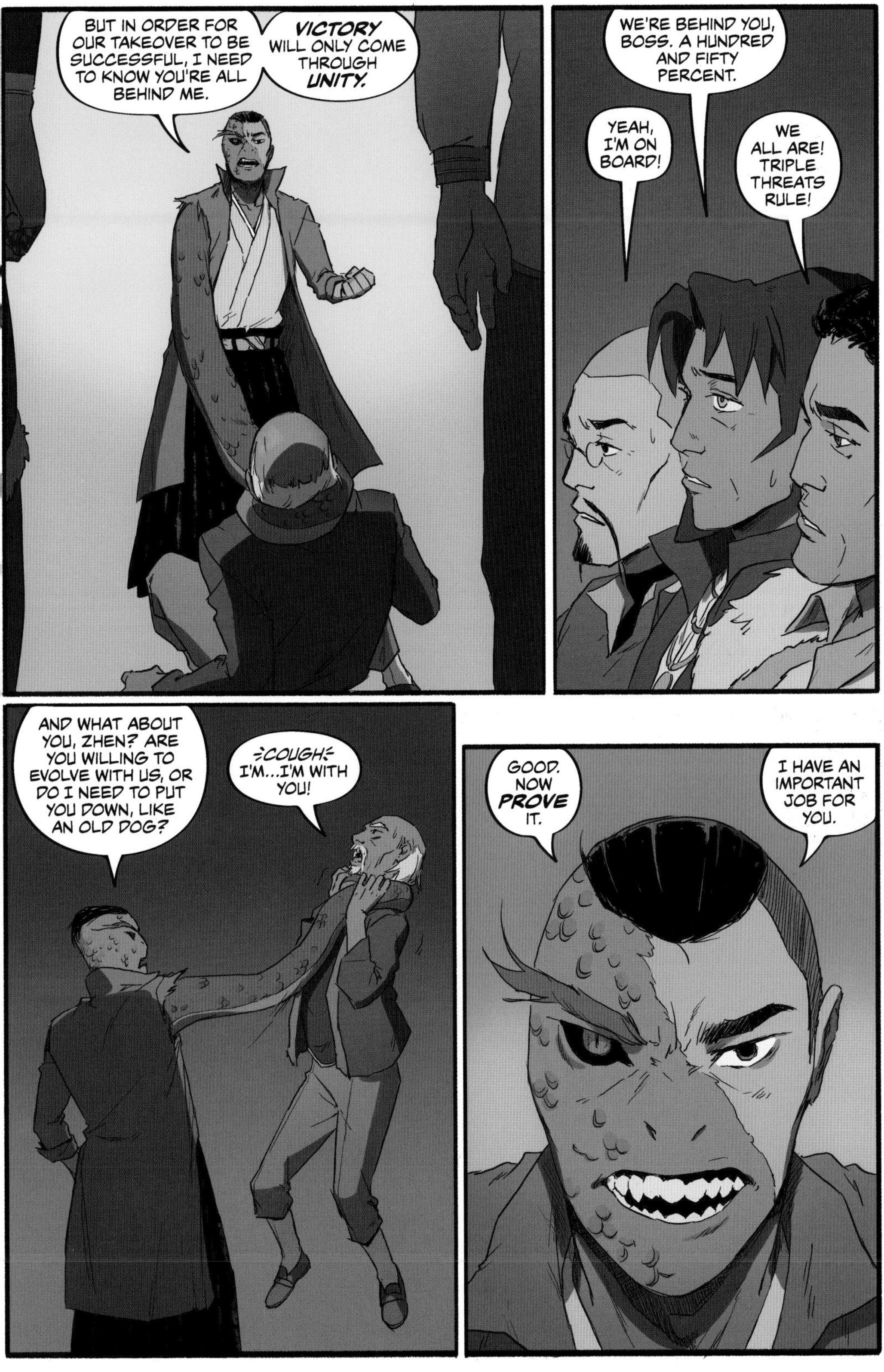
BUT IN ORDER FOR OUR TAKEOVER TO BE SUCCESSFUL, I NEED TO KNOW YOU'RE ALL BEHIND ME.
VICTORY WILL ONLY COME THROUGH UNITY.
WE'RE BEHIND YOU, BOSS. A HUNDRED AND FIFTY PERCENT.
YEAH, I'M ON BOARD!
WE ALL ARE! TRIPLE THREATS RULE!
AND WHAT ABOUT YOU, ZHEN? ARE YOU WILLING TO EVOLVE WITH US, OR DO I NEED TO PUT YOU DOWN, LIKE AN OLD DOG?
COUGH I'M...I'M WITH YOU!
GOOD. NOW PROVE IT.
I HAVE AN IMPORTANT JOB FOR YOU.

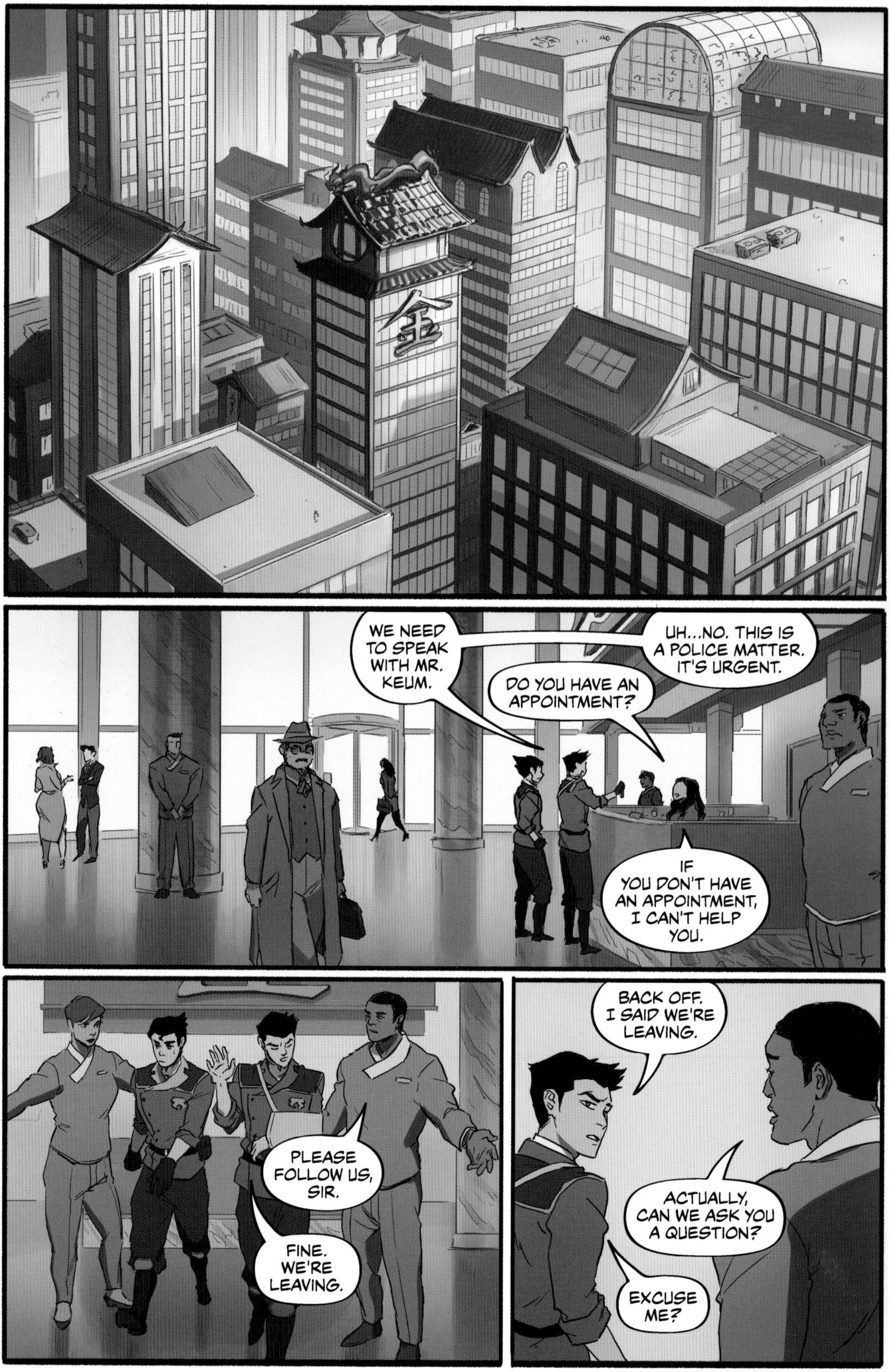

WE NEED TO SPEAK WITH MR. KEUM.
DO YOU HAVE AN APPOINTMENT?
UH...NO. THIS IS A POLICE MATTER. IT'S URGENT.
IF YOU DON'T HAVE AN APPOINTMENT, I CAN'T HELP YOU.
PLEASE FOLLOW US, SIR.
FINE. WE'RE LEAVING.
BACK OFF. I SAID WE'RE LEAVING.
ACTUALLY, CAN WE ASK YOU A QUESTION?
EXCUSE ME?

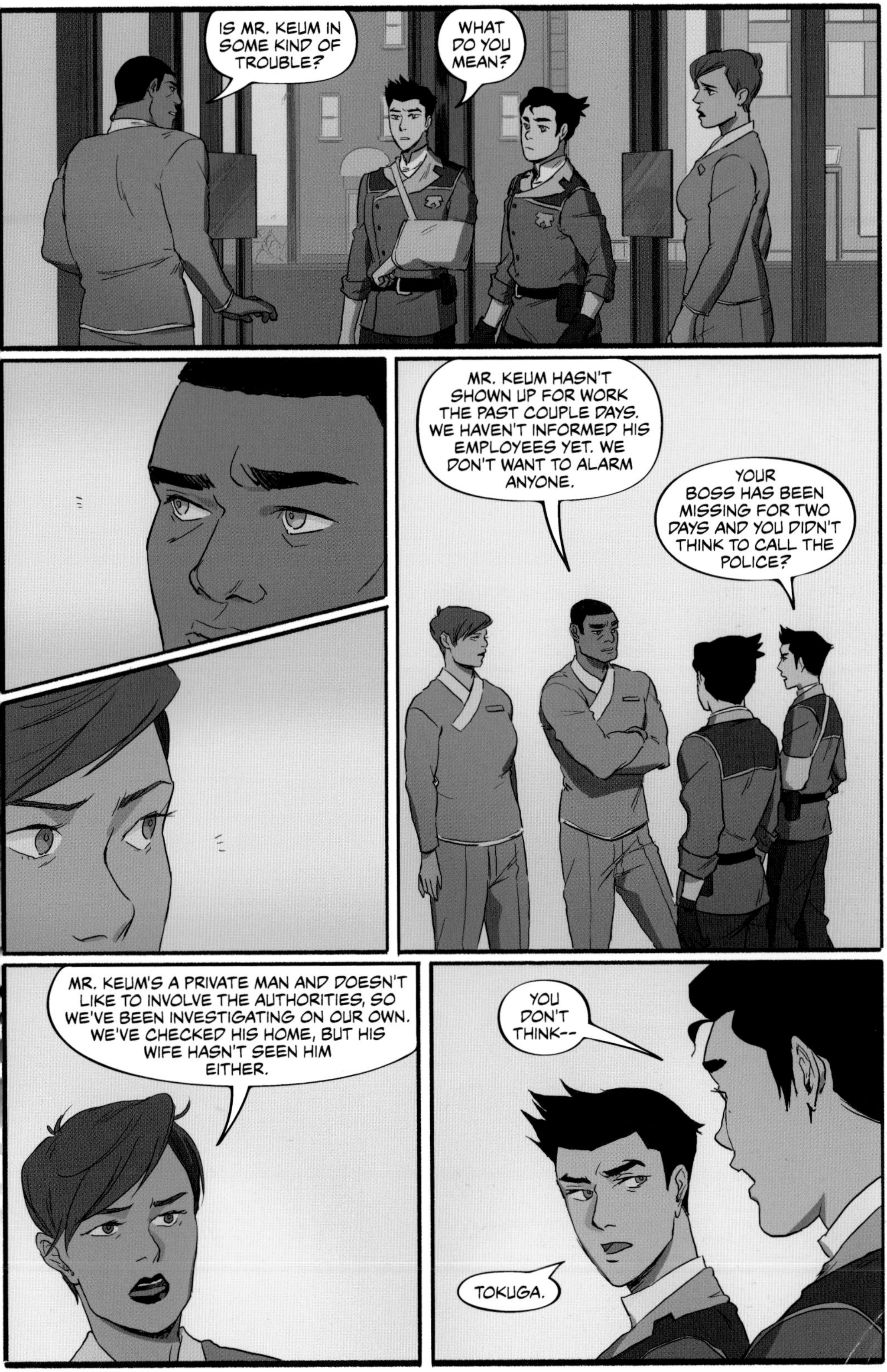
IS MR. KEUM IN SOME KIND OF TROUBLE?
WHAT DO YOU MEAN?
MR. KEUM HASN'T SHOWN UP FOR WORK THE PAST COUPLE DAYS. WE HAVEN'T INFORMED HIS EMPLOYEES YET. WE DON'T WANT TO ALARM ANYONE.
YOUR BOSS HAS BEEN MISSING FOR TWO DAYS AND YOU DIDN'T THINK TO CALL THE POLICE?
MR. KEUM'S A PRIVATE MAN AND DOESN'T LIKE TO INVOLVE THE AUTHORITIES, SO WE'VE BEEN INVESTIGATING ON OUR OWN. WE'VE CHECKED HIS HOME, BUT HIS WIFE HASN'T SEEN HIM EITHER.
YOU DON'T THINK--
TOKUGA.

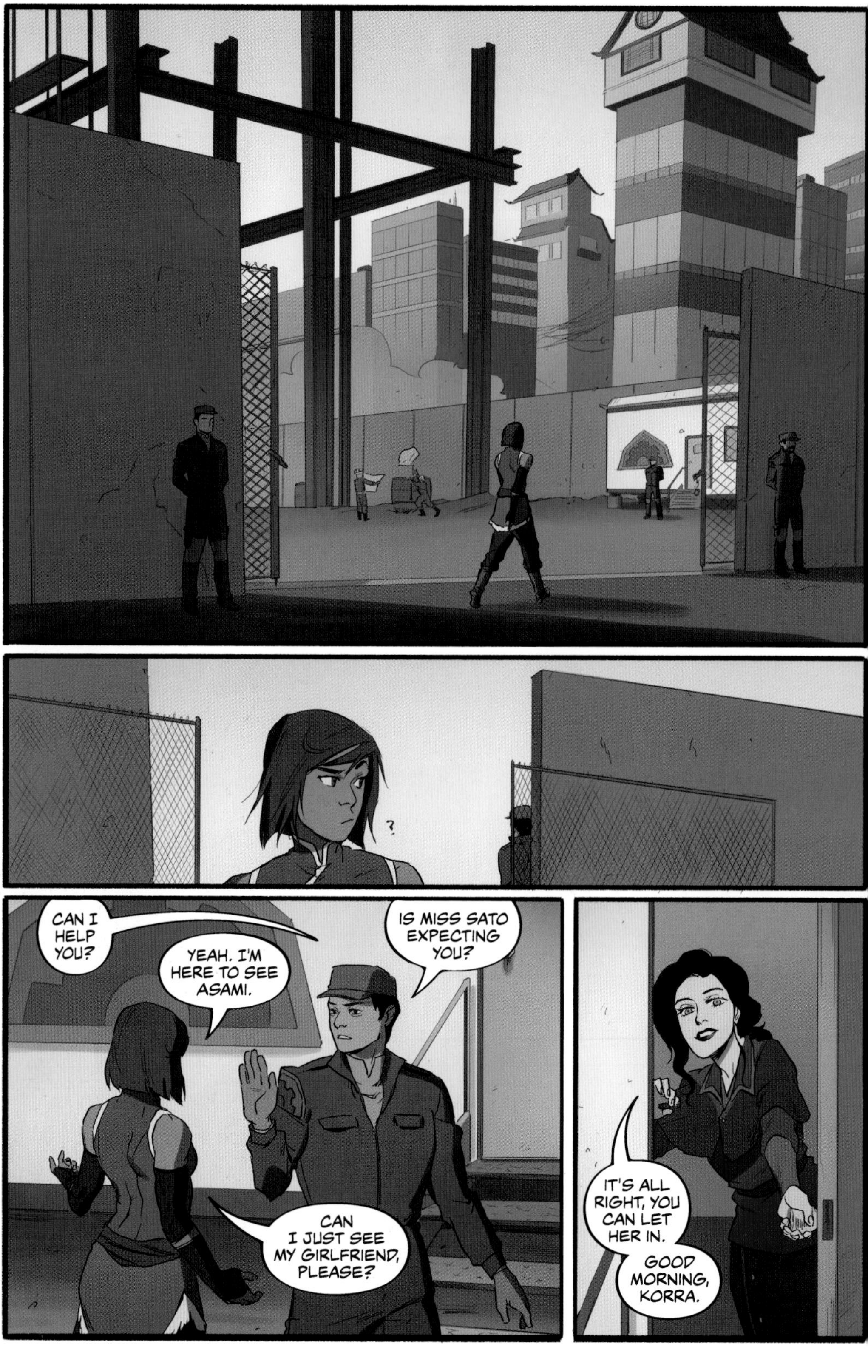
?
CAN I HELP YOU?
YEAH. I'M HERE TO SEE ASAMI.
IS MISS SATO EXPECTING YOU?
CAN I JUST SEE MY GIRLFRIEND, PLEASE?
IT'S ALL RIGHT, YOU CAN LET HER IN.
GOOD MORNING, KORRA.

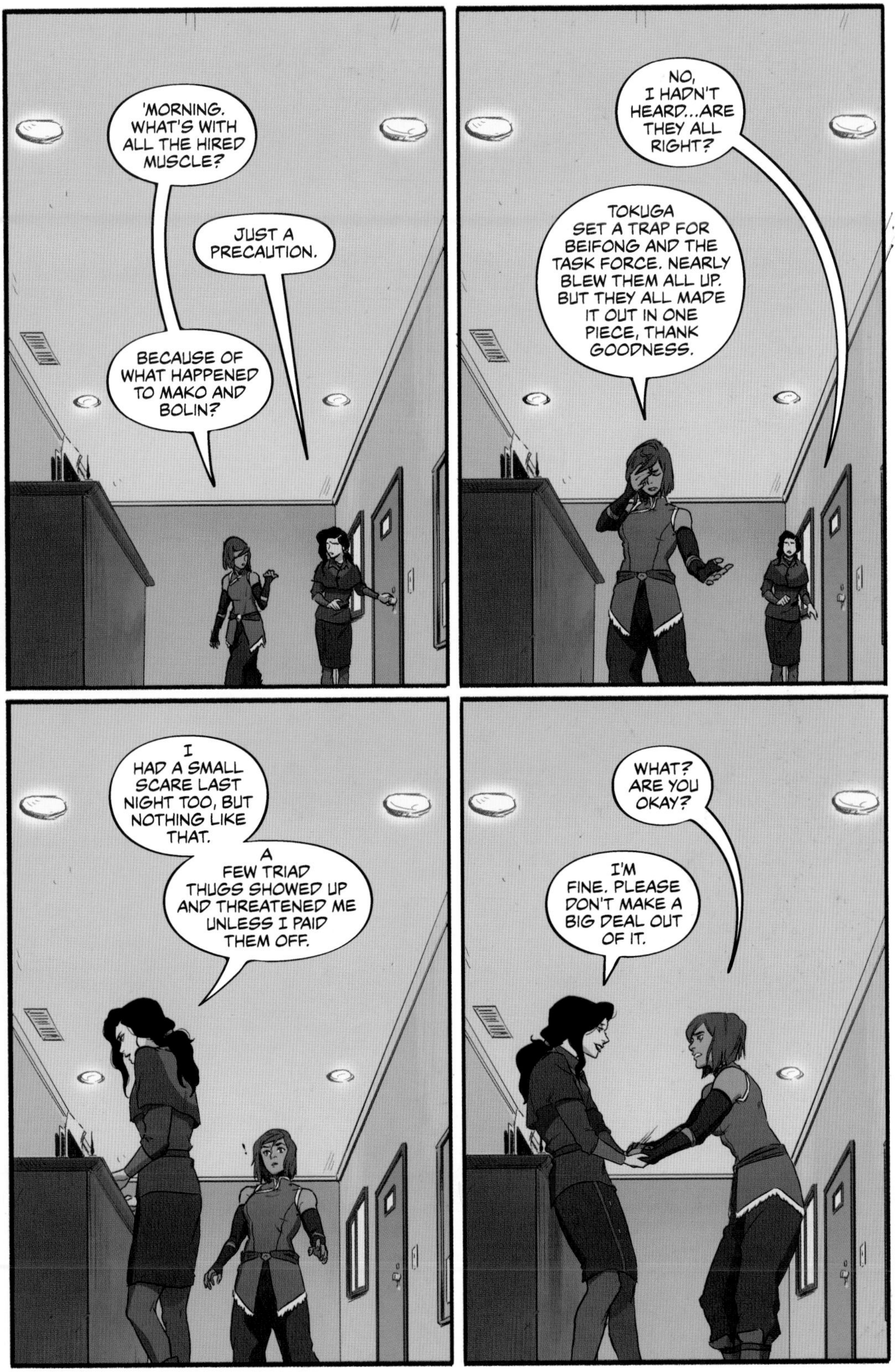
'MORNING. WHAT'S WITH ALL THE HIRED MUSCLE?
JUST A PRECAUTION.
BECAUSE OF WHAT HAPPENED TO MAKO AND BOLIN?
NO, I HADN'T HEARD...ARE THEY ALL RIGHT?
TOKUGA SET A TRAP FOR BEIFONG AND THE TASK FORCE. NEARLY BLEW THEM ALL UP. BUT THEY ALL MADE IT OUT IN ONE PIECE, THANK GOODNESS.
I HAD A SMALL SCARE LAST NIGHT TOO, BUT NOTHING LIKE THAT.
A FEW TRIAD THUGS SHOWED UP AND THREATENED ME UNLESS I PAID THEM OFF.
WHAT? ARE YOU OKAY?
I'M FINE. PLEASE DON'T MAKE A BIG DEAL OUT OF IT.

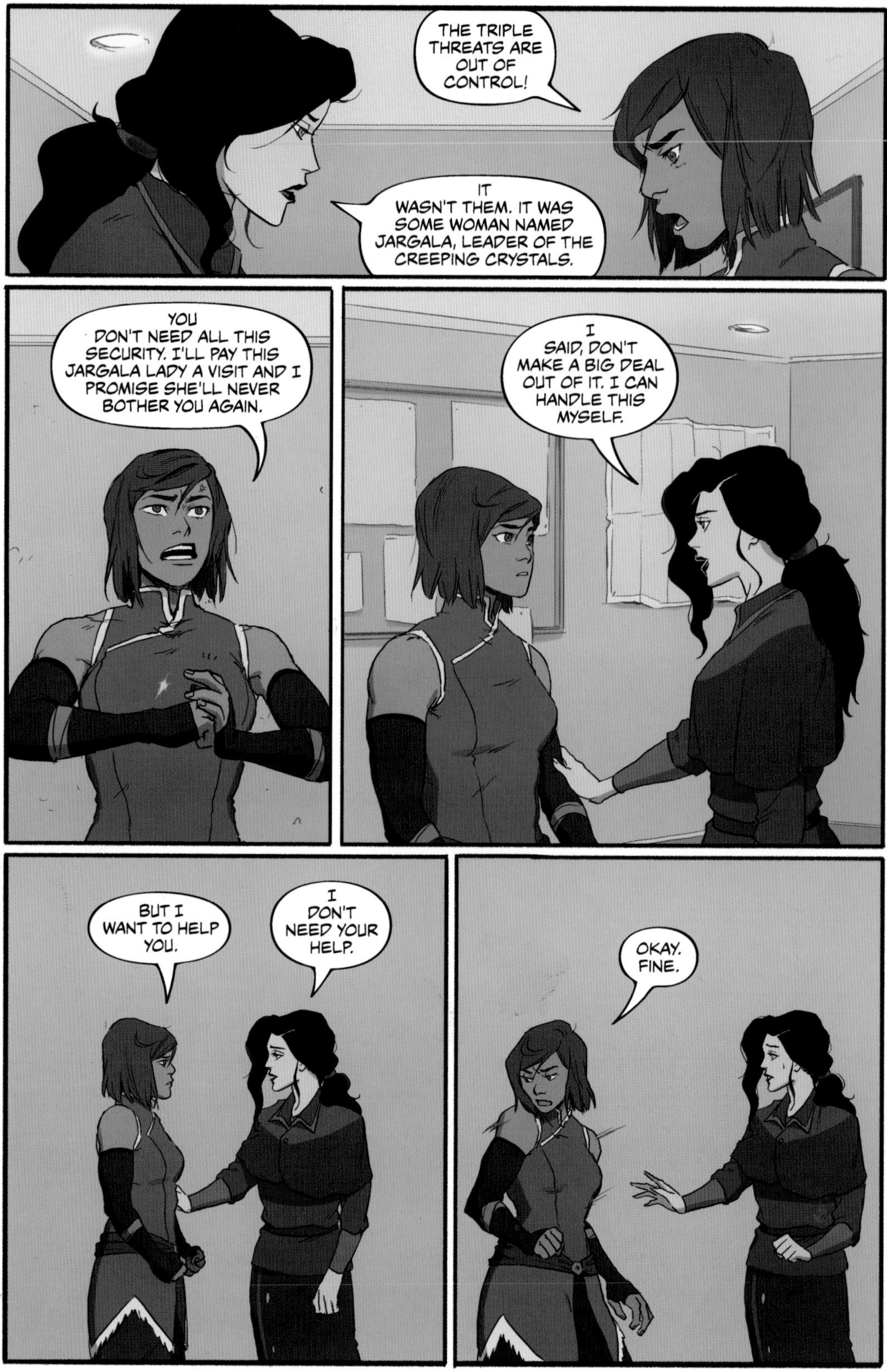
THE TRIPLE THREATS ARE OUT OF CONTROL!
IT WASN'T THEM. IT WAS SOME WOMAN NAMED JARGALA, LEADER OF THE CREEPING CRYSTALS.
YOU DON'T NEED ALL THIS SECURITY. I'LL PAY THIS JARGALA LADY A VISIT AND I PROMISE SHE'LL NEVER BOTHER YOU AGAIN.
I SAID, DON'T MAKE A BIG DEAL OUT OF IT. I CAN HANDLE THIS MYSELF.
BUT I WANT TO HELP YOU.
I DON'T NEED YOUR HELP.
OKAY. FINE.

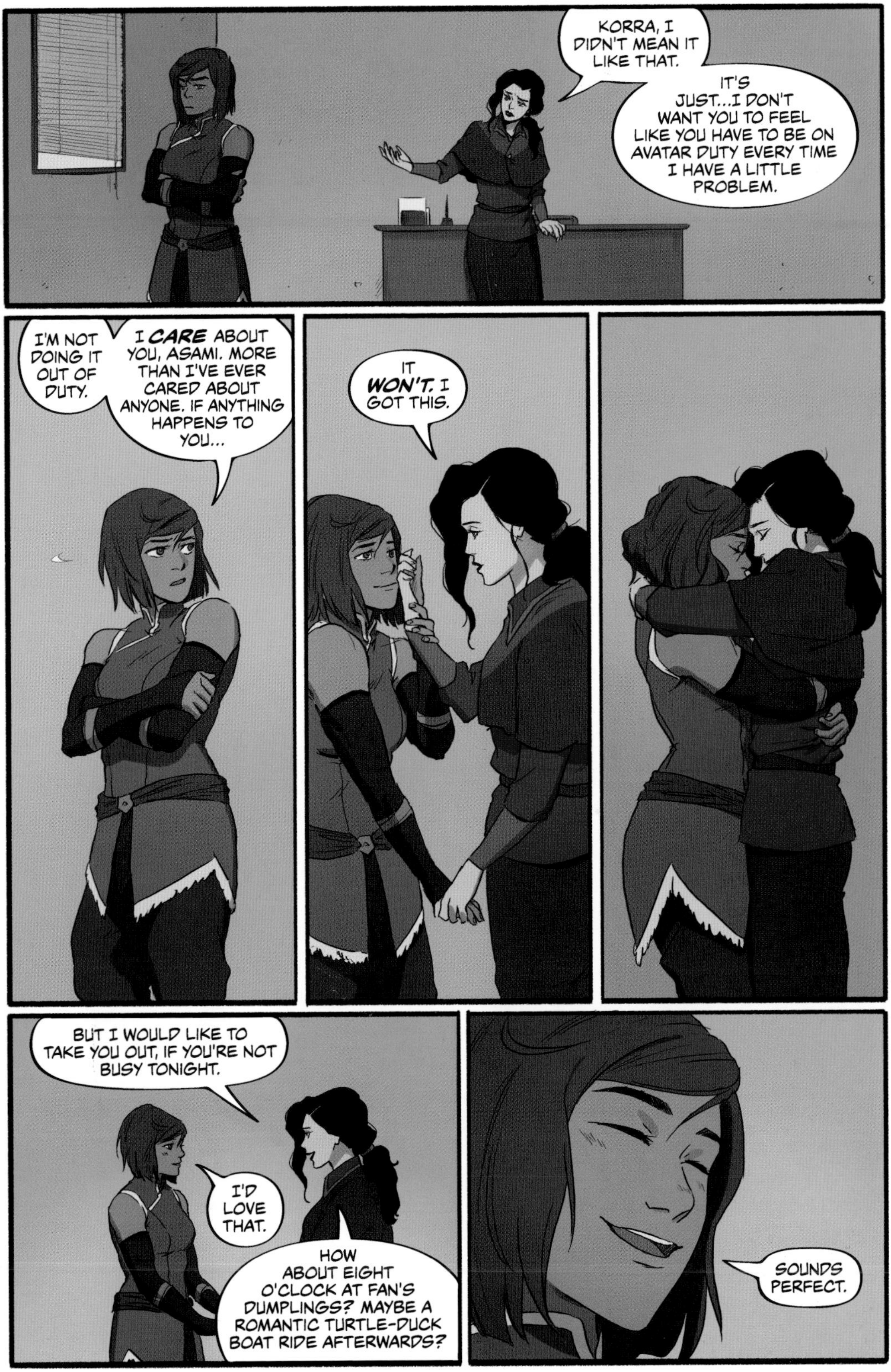
KORRA, I DIDN'T MEAN IT LIKE THAT.
IT'S JUST...I DON'T WANT YOU TO FEEL LIKE YOU HAVE TO BE ON AVATAR DUTY EVERY TIME I HAVE A LITTLE PROBLEM.
I'M NOT DOING IT OUT OF DUTY.
I CARE ABOUT YOU, ASAMI. MORE THAN I'VE EVER CARED ABOUT ANYONE. IF ANYTHING HAPPENS TO YOU...
IT WON'T. I GOT THIS.
BUT I WOULD LIKE TO TAKE YOU OUT, IF YOU'RE NOT BUSY TONIGHT.
I'D LOVE THAT.
HOW ABOUT EIGHT O'CLOCK AT FAN'S DUMPLINGS? MAYBE A ROMANTIC TURTLE-DUCK BOAT RIDE AFTERWARDS?
SOUNDS PERFECT.

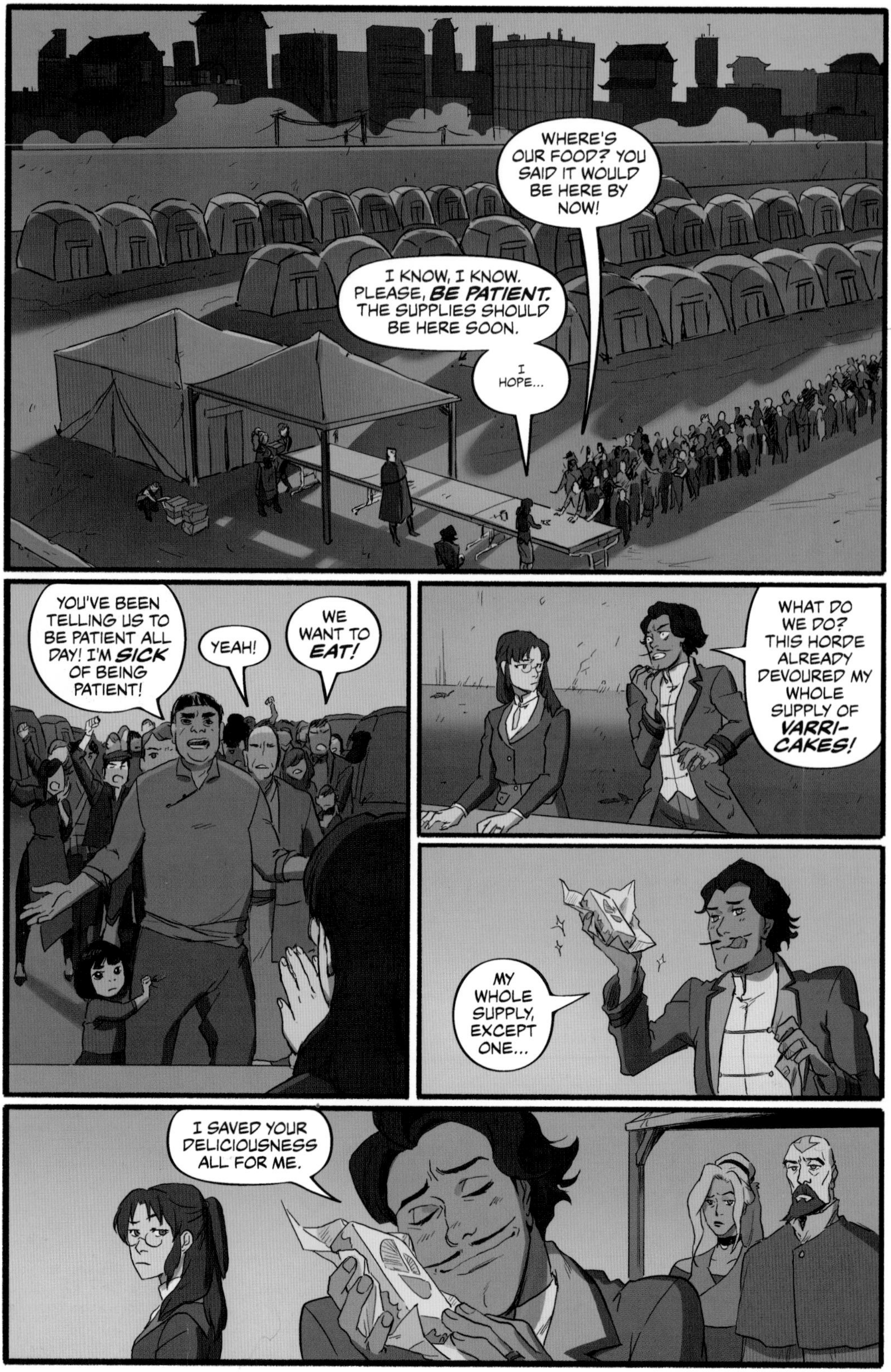
WHERE'S OUR FOOD? YOU SAID IT WOULD BE HERE BY NOW!
I KNOW, I KNOW. PLEASE, BE PATIENT. THE SUPPLIES SHOULD BE HERE SOON.
I HOPE...
YOU'VE BEEN TELLING US TO BE PATIENT ALL DAY! I'M SICK OF BEING PATIENT!
YEAH!
WE WANT TO EAT!
WHAT DO WE DO? THIS HORDE ALREADY DEVOURED MY WHOLE SUPPLY OF VARRI-CAKES!
MY WHOLE SUPPLY, EXCEPT ONE...
I SAVED YOUR DELICIOUSNESS ALL FOR ME.

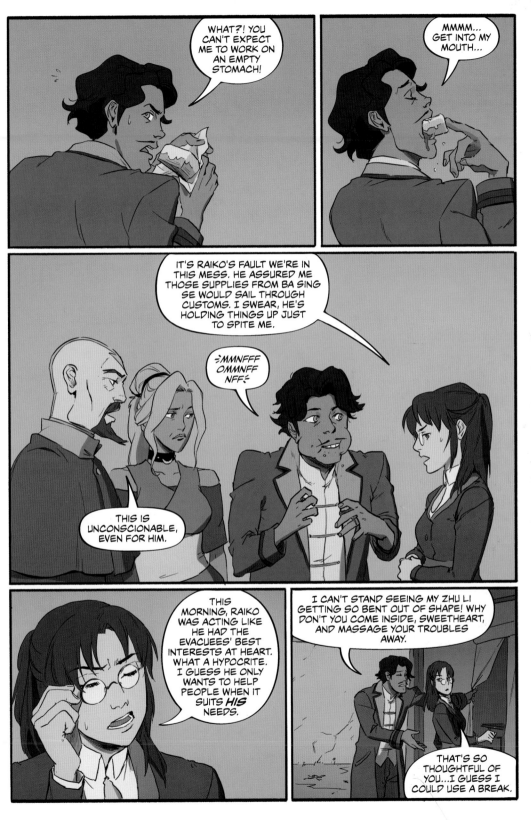

WHAT?! YOU CAN'T EXPECT ME TO WORK ON AN EMPTY STOMACH!

MMMM... GET INTO MY MOUTH...

IT'S RAIKO'S FAULT WE'RE IN THIS MESS. HE ASSURED ME THOSE SUPPLIES FROM BA SING SE WOULD SAIL THROUGH CUSTOMS. I SWEAR, HE'S HOLDING THINGS UP JUST TO SPITE ME.

≶MMNFFF OMMNFF NFF≶

THIS IS UNCONSCIONABLE, EVEN FOR HIM.

THIS MORNING, RAIKO WAS ACTING LIKE HE HAD THE EVACUEES' BEST INTERESTS AT HEART. WHAT A HYPOCRITE. I GUESS HE ONLY WANTS TO HELP PEOPLE WHEN IT SUITS *HIS* NEEDS.

I CAN'T STAND SEEING MY ZHU LI GETTING SO BENT OUT OF SHAPE! WHY DON'T YOU COME INSIDE, SWEETHEART, AND MASSAGE YOUR TROUBLES AWAY.

THAT'S SO THOUGHTFUL OF YOU...I GUESS I COULD USE A BREAK.

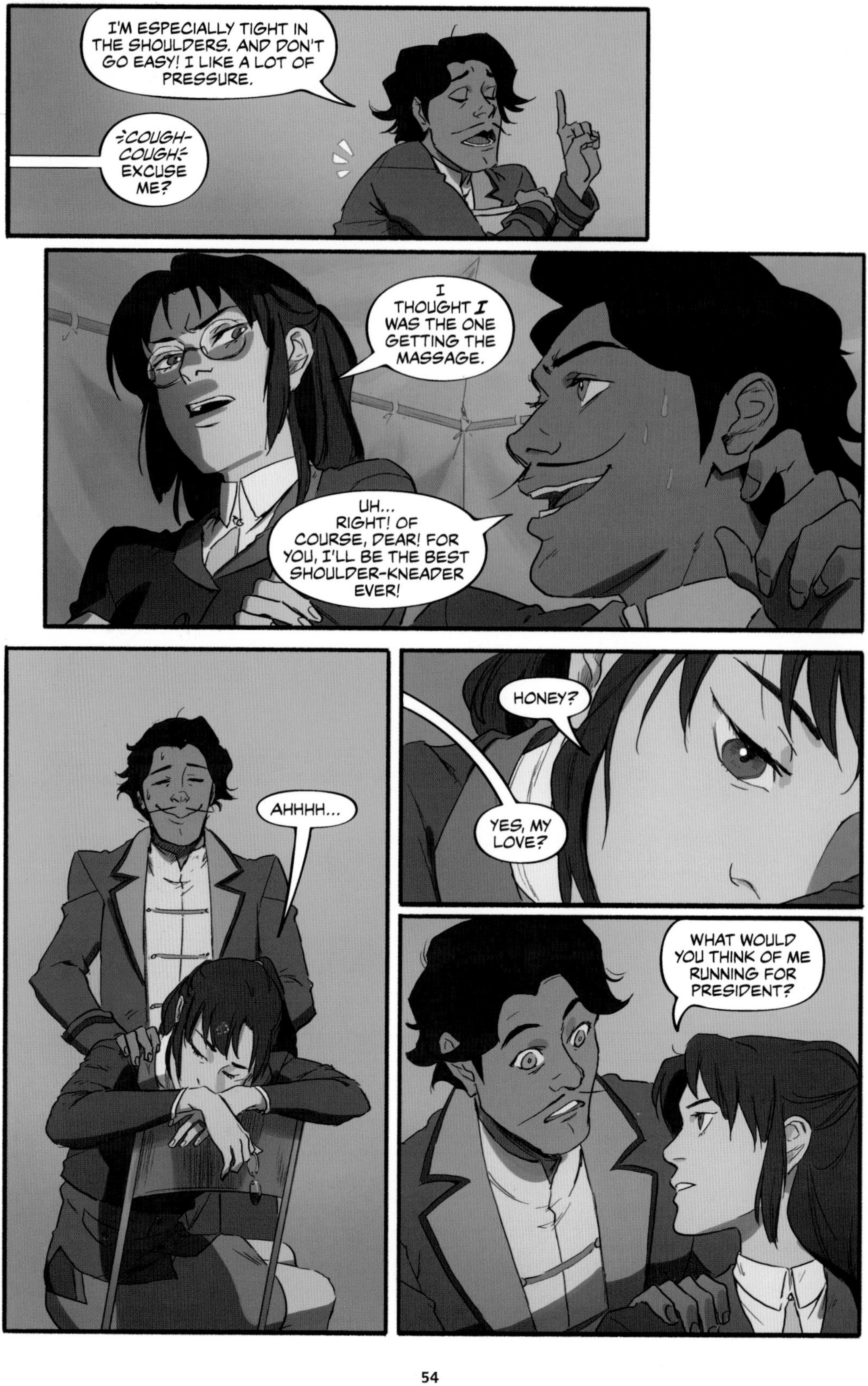
I'M ESPECIALLY TIGHT IN THE SHOULDERS. AND DON'T GO EASY! I LIKE A LOT OF PRESSURE.
-COUGH-COUGH- EXCUSE ME?
I THOUGHT I WAS THE ONE GETTING THE MASSAGE.
UH... RIGHT! OF COURSE, DEAR! FOR YOU, I'LL BE THE BEST SHOULDER-KNEADER EVER!
AHHHH...
HONEY?
YES, MY LOVE?
WHAT WOULD YOU THINK OF ME RUNNING FOR PRESIDENT?

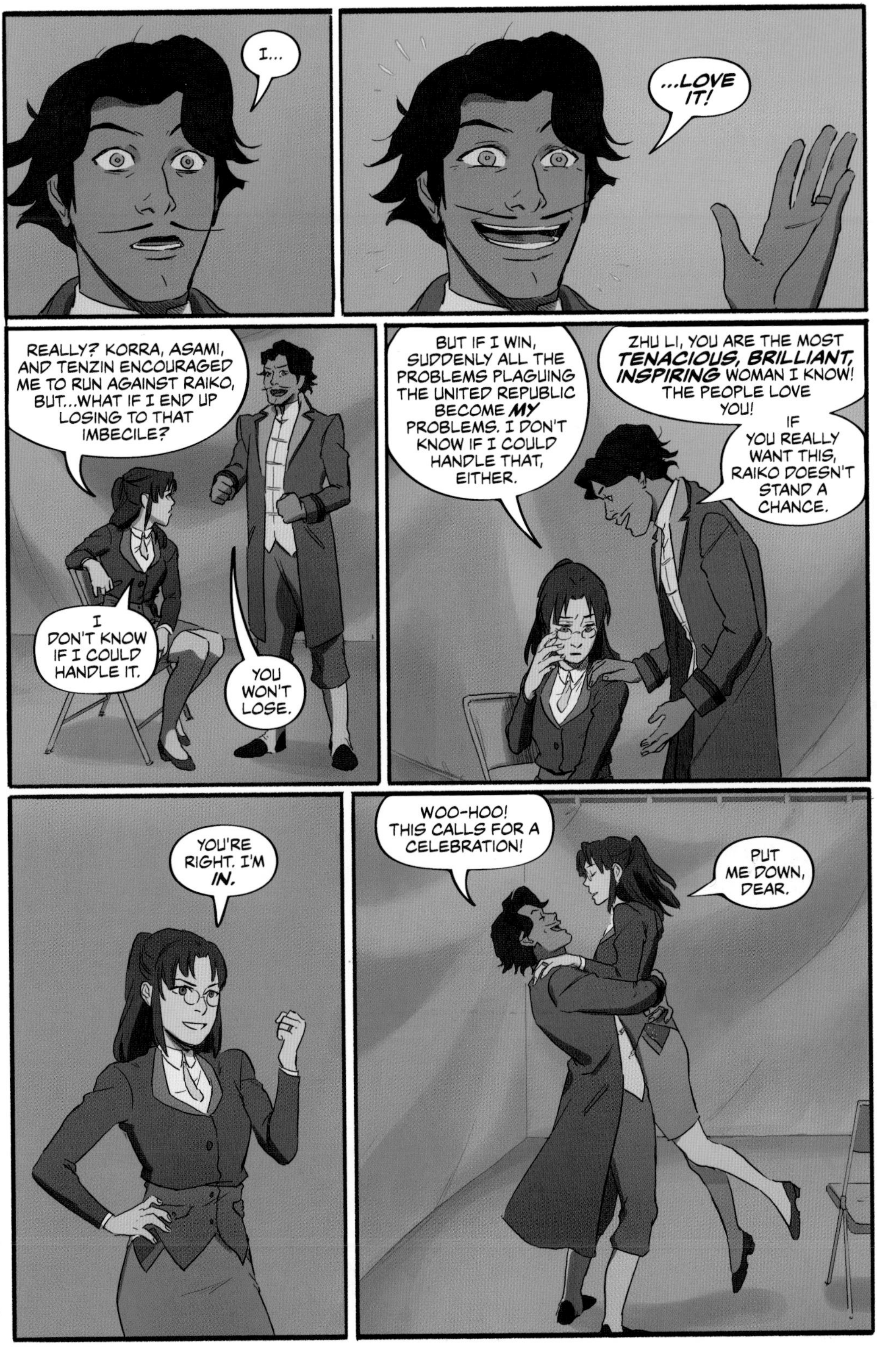
I...
...LOVE IT!
REALLY? KORRA, ASAMI, AND TENZIN ENCOURAGED ME TO RUN AGAINST RAIKO, BUT...WHAT IF I END UP LOSING TO THAT IMBECILE?
I DON'T KNOW IF I COULD HANDLE IT.
YOU WON'T LOSE.
BUT IF I WIN, SUDDENLY ALL THE PROBLEMS PLAGUING THE UNITED REPUBLIC BECOME MY PROBLEMS. I DON'T KNOW IF I COULD HANDLE THAT, EITHER.
ZHU LI, YOU ARE THE MOST TENACIOUS, BRILLIANT, INSPIRING WOMAN I KNOW! THE PEOPLE LOVE YOU!
IF YOU REALLY WANT THIS, RAIKO DOESN'T STAND A CHANCE.
YOU'RE RIGHT. I'M IN.
WOO-HOO! THIS CALLS FOR A CELEBRATION!
PUT ME DOWN, DEAR.

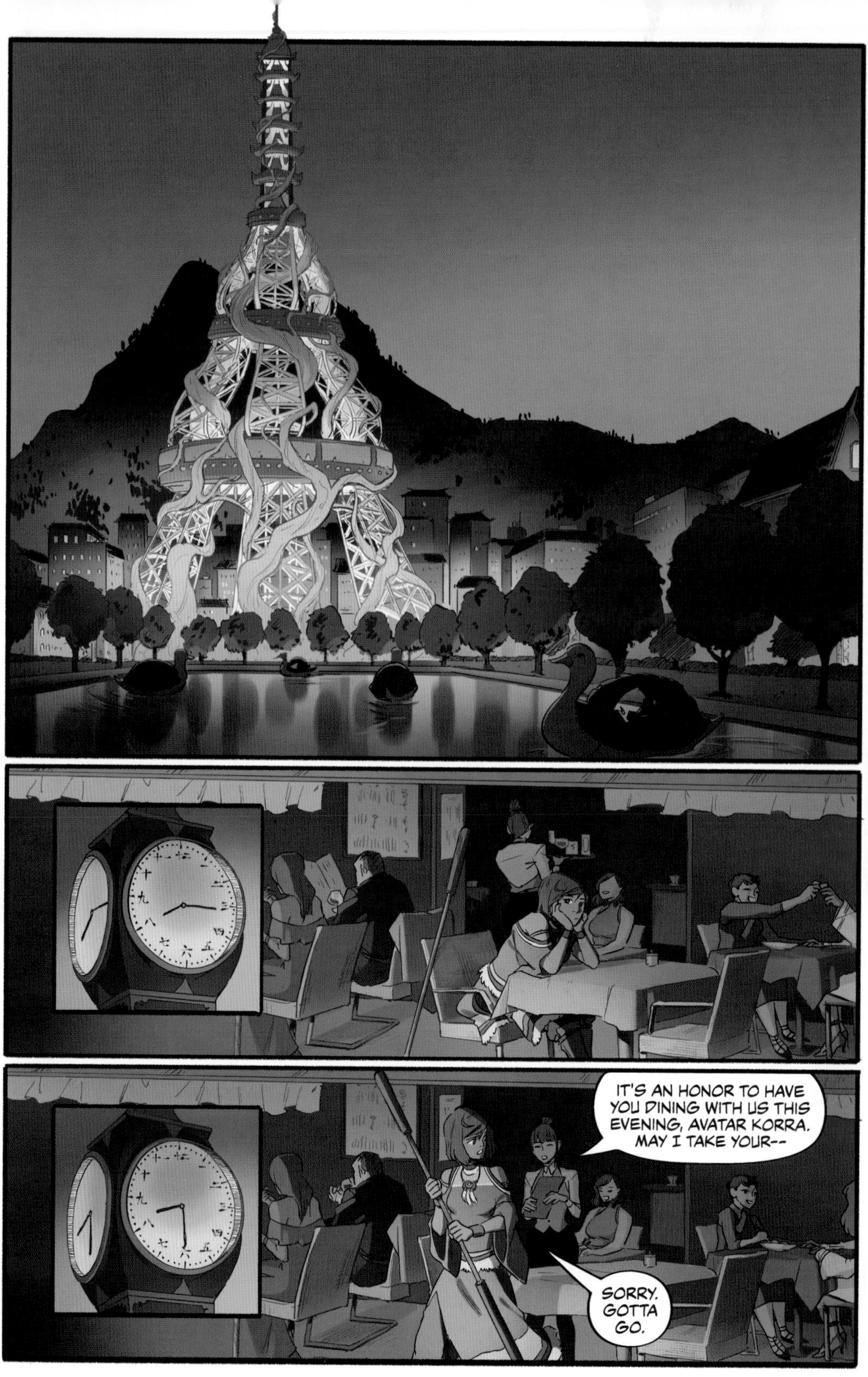
IT'S AN HONOR TO HAVE YOU DINING WITH US THIS EVENING, AVATAR KORRA. MAY I TAKE YOUR--
SORRY. GOTTA GO.

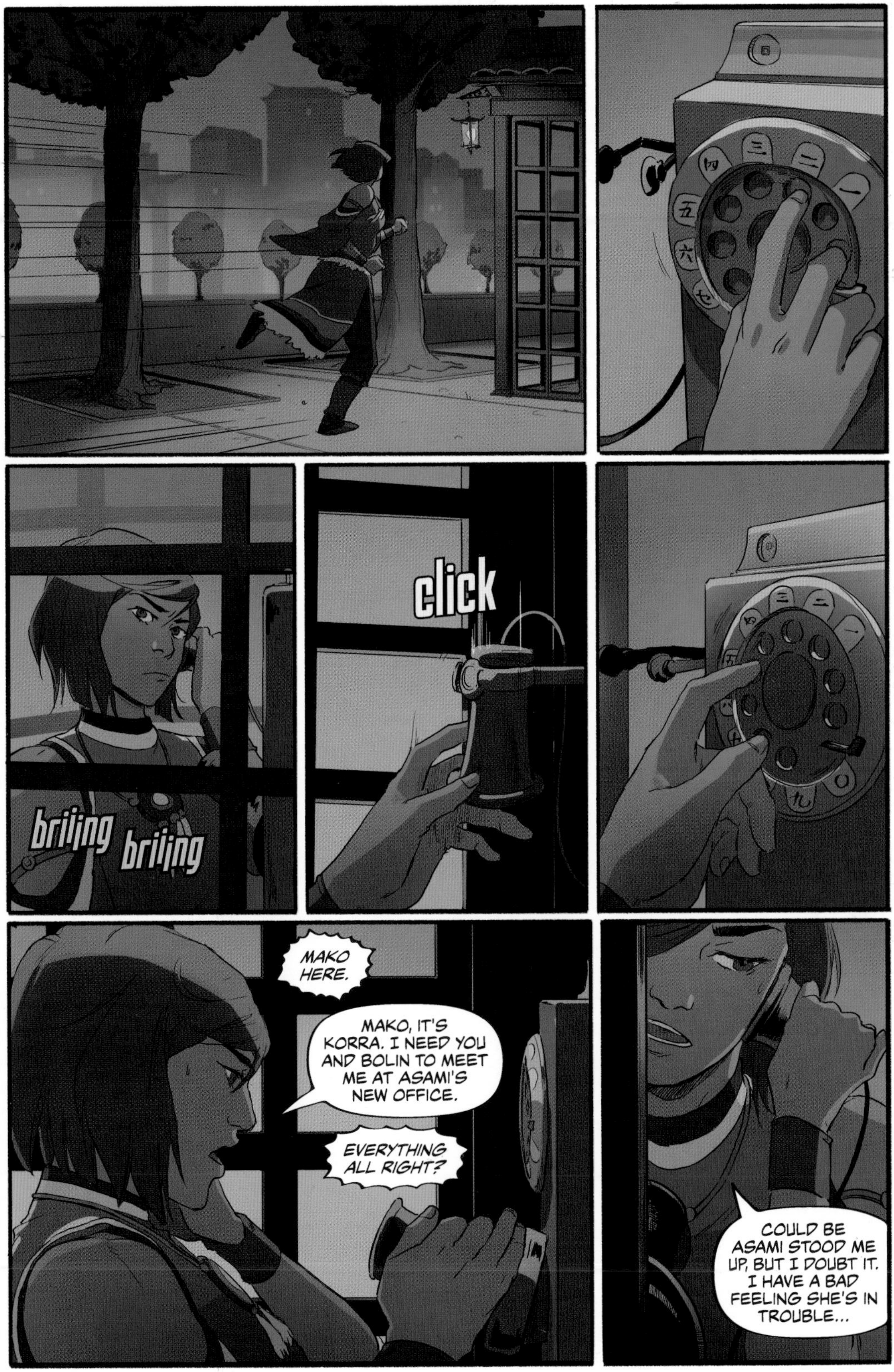

briiing briiing
click
MAKO HERE.
MAKO, IT'S KORRA. I NEED YOU AND BOLIN TO MEET ME AT ASAMI'S NEW OFFICE.
EVERYTHING ALL RIGHT?
COULD BE ASAMI STOOD ME UP, BUT I DOUBT IT. I HAVE A BAD FEELING SHE'S IN TROUBLE...

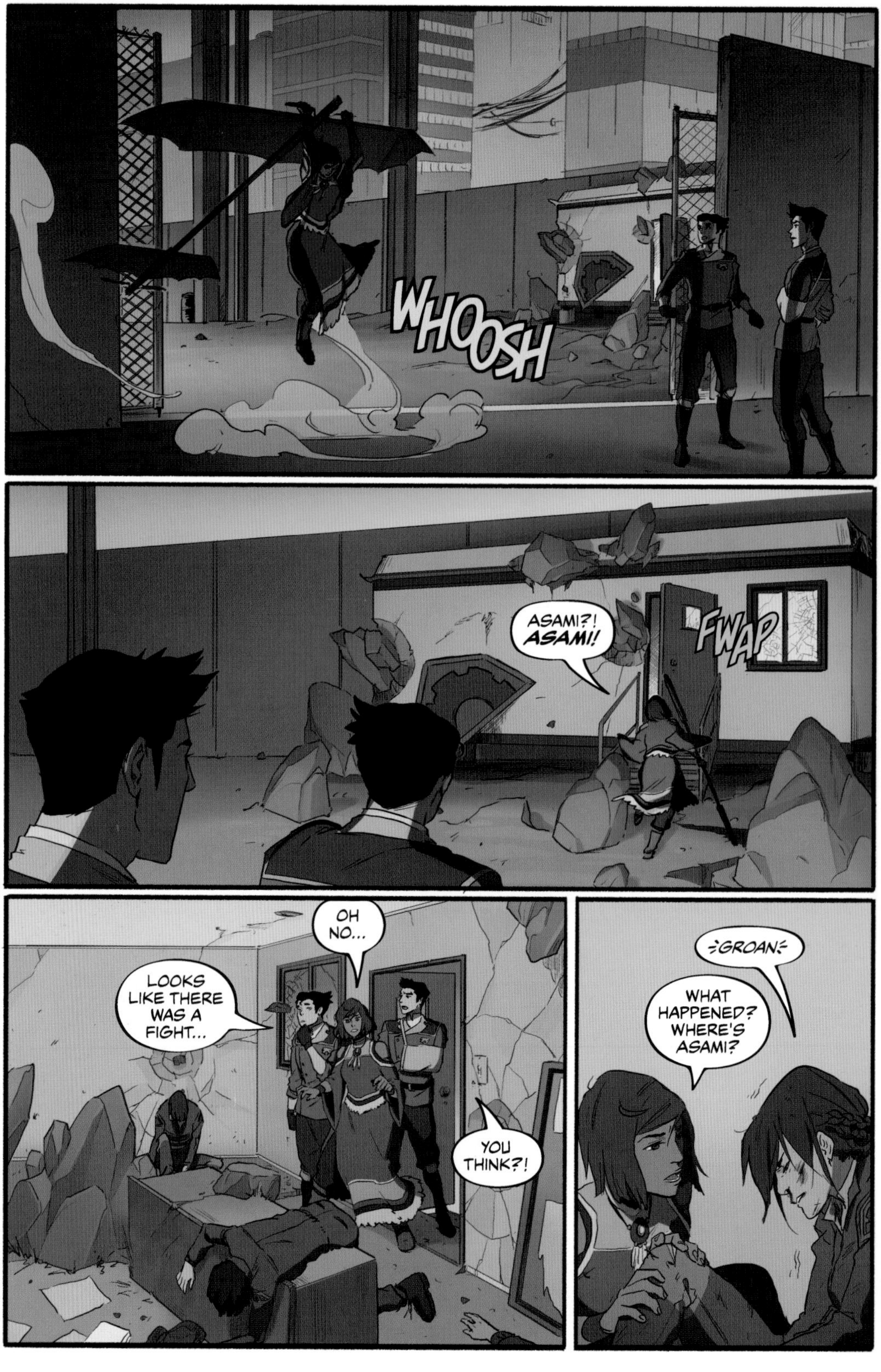
WHOOSH
ASAMI?! ASAMI!
FWAP
OH NO...
LOOKS LIKE THERE WAS A FIGHT...
YOU THINK?!
GROAN
WHAT HAPPENED? WHERE'S ASAMI?

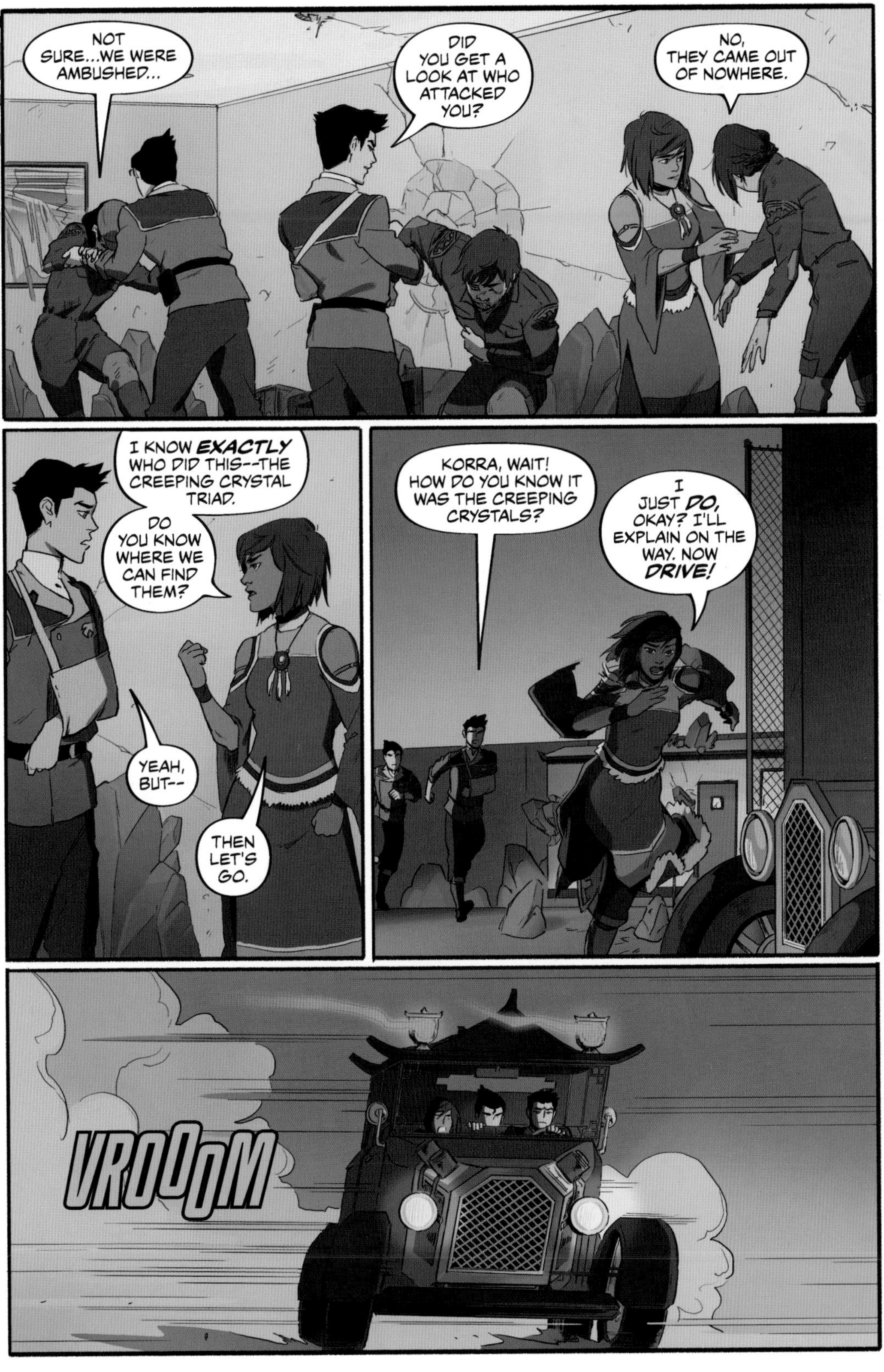
NOT SURE...WE WERE AMBUSHED...
DID YOU GET A LOOK AT WHO ATTACKED YOU?
NO, THEY CAME OUT OF NOWHERE.
I KNOW EXACTLY WHO DID THIS--THE CREEPING CRYSTAL TRIAD.
DO YOU KNOW WHERE WE CAN FIND THEM?
YEAH, BUT--
THEN LET'S GO.
KORRA, WAIT! HOW DO YOU KNOW IT WAS THE CREEPING CRYSTALS?
I JUST DO, OKAY? I'LL EXPLAIN ON THE WAY. NOW DRIVE!
VROOOOM

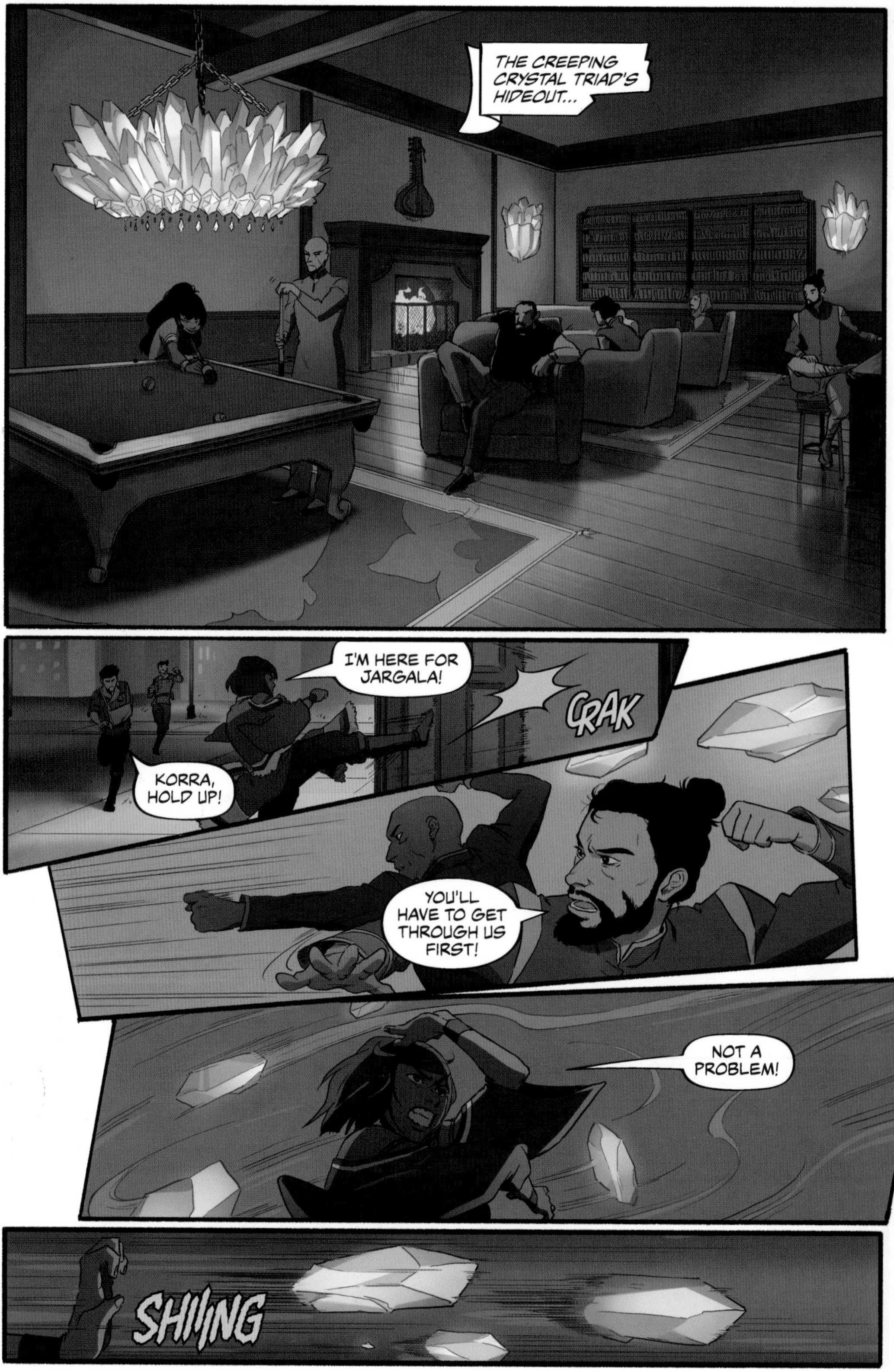
THE CREEPING CRYSTAL TRIAD'S HIDEOUT...
I'M HERE FOR JARGALA!
CRAK
KORRA, HOLD UP!
YOU'LL HAVE TO GET THROUGH US FIRST!
NOT A PROBLEM!
SHIING

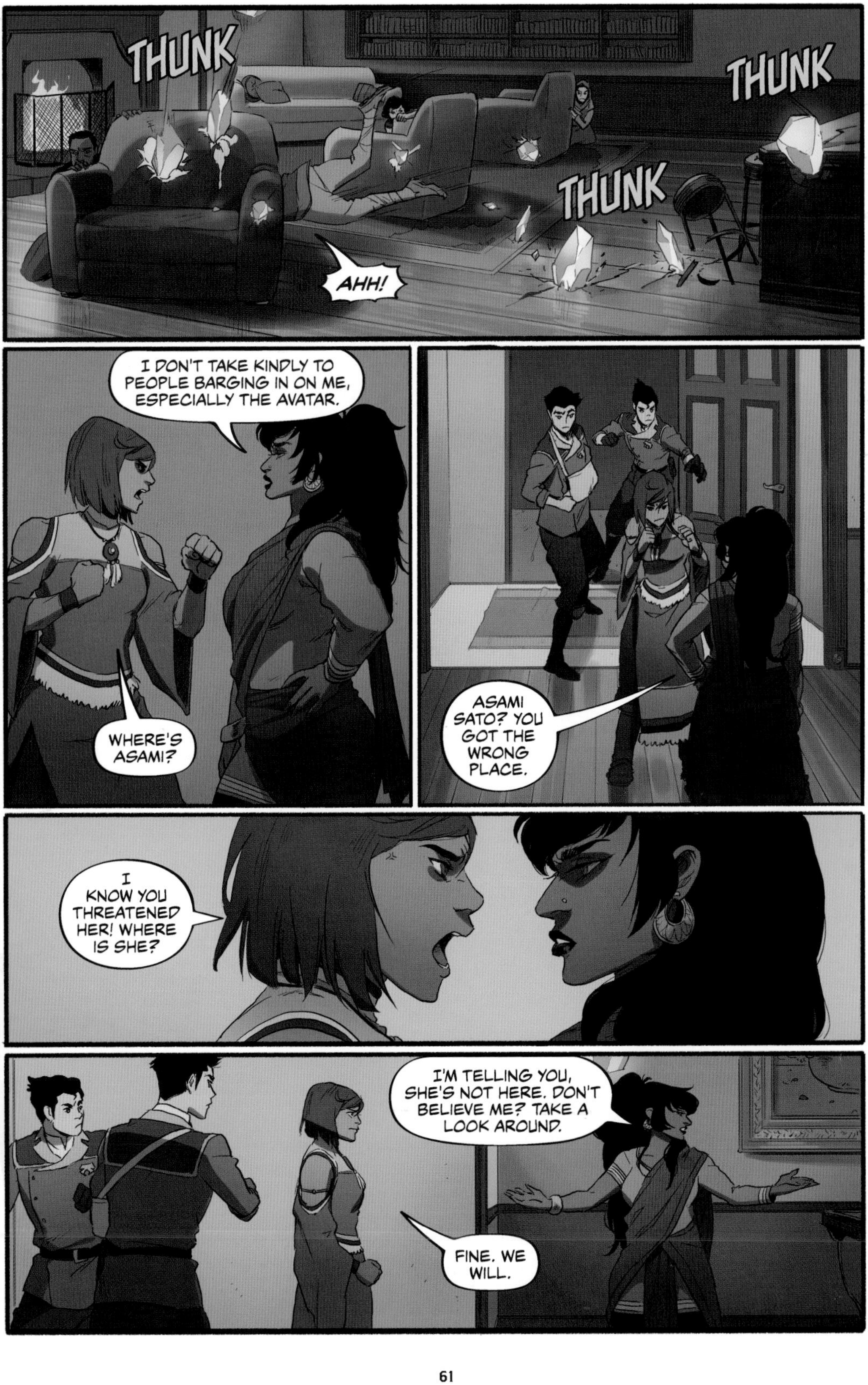
THUNK
THUNK
THUNK
AHH!
I DON'T TAKE KINDLY TO PEOPLE BARGING IN ON ME, ESPECIALLY THE AVATAR.
WHERE'S ASAMI?
ASAMI SATO? YOU GOT THE WRONG PLACE.
I KNOW YOU THREATENED HER! WHERE IS SHE?
I'M TELLING YOU, SHE'S NOT HERE. DON'T BELIEVE ME? TAKE A LOOK AROUND.
FINE. WE WILL.

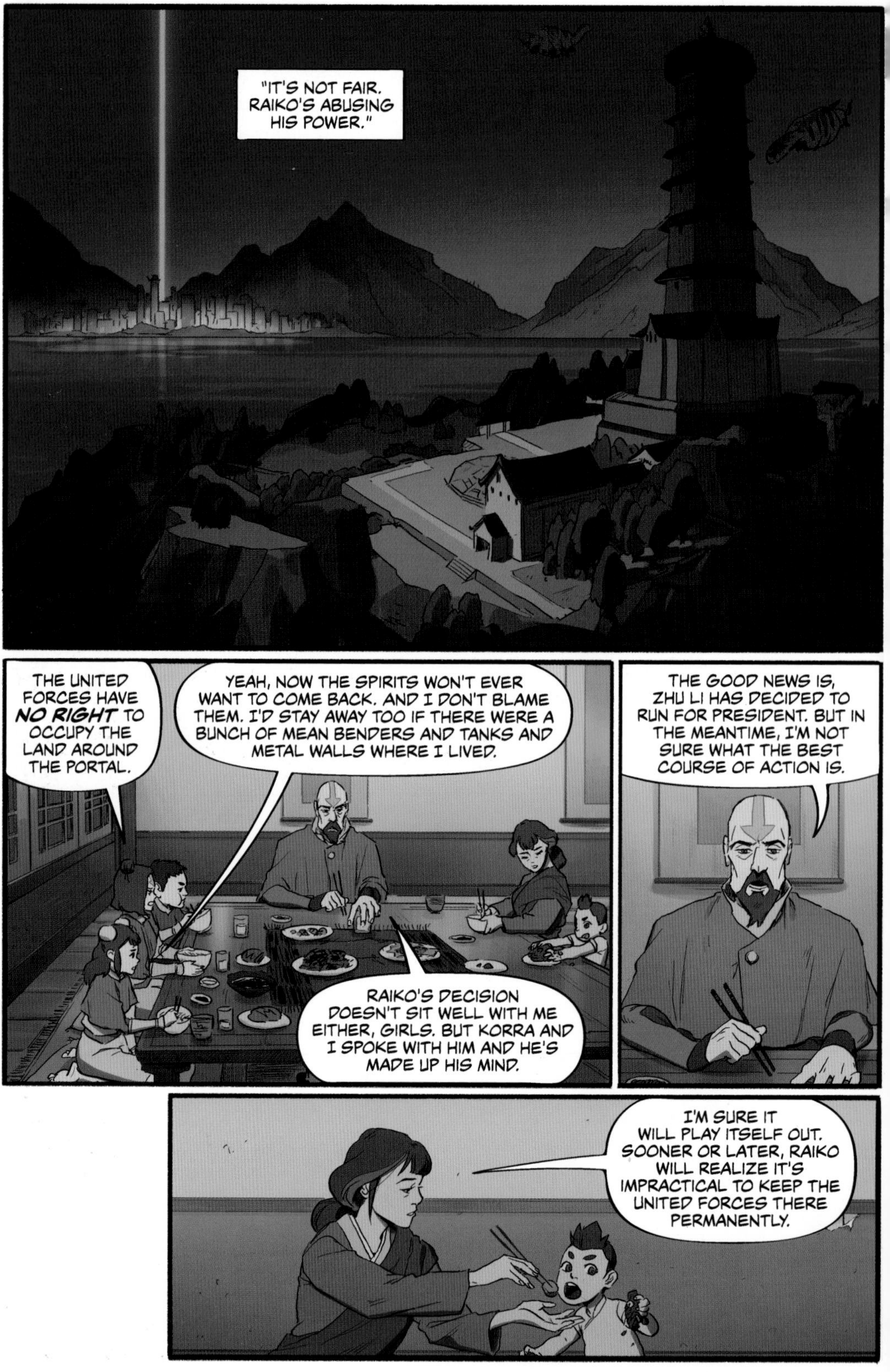
"IT'S NOT FAIR. RAIKO'S ABUSING HIS POWER."
THE UNITED FORCES HAVE ***NO RIGHT*** TO OCCUPY THE LAND AROUND THE PORTAL.
YEAH, NOW THE SPIRITS WON'T EVER WANT TO COME BACK. AND I DON'T BLAME THEM. I'D STAY AWAY TOO IF THERE WERE A BUNCH OF MEAN BENDERS AND TANKS AND METAL WALLS WHERE I LIVED.
RAIKO'S DECISION DOESN'T SIT WELL WITH ME EITHER, GIRLS. BUT KORRA AND I SPOKE WITH HIM AND HE'S MADE UP HIS MIND.
THE GOOD NEWS IS, ZHU LI HAS DECIDED TO RUN FOR PRESIDENT. BUT IN THE MEANTIME, I'M NOT SURE WHAT THE BEST COURSE OF ACTION IS.
I'M SURE IT WILL PLAY ITSELF OUT. SOONER OR LATER, RAIKO WILL REALIZE IT'S IMPRACTICAL TO KEEP THE UNITED FORCES THERE PERMANENTLY.

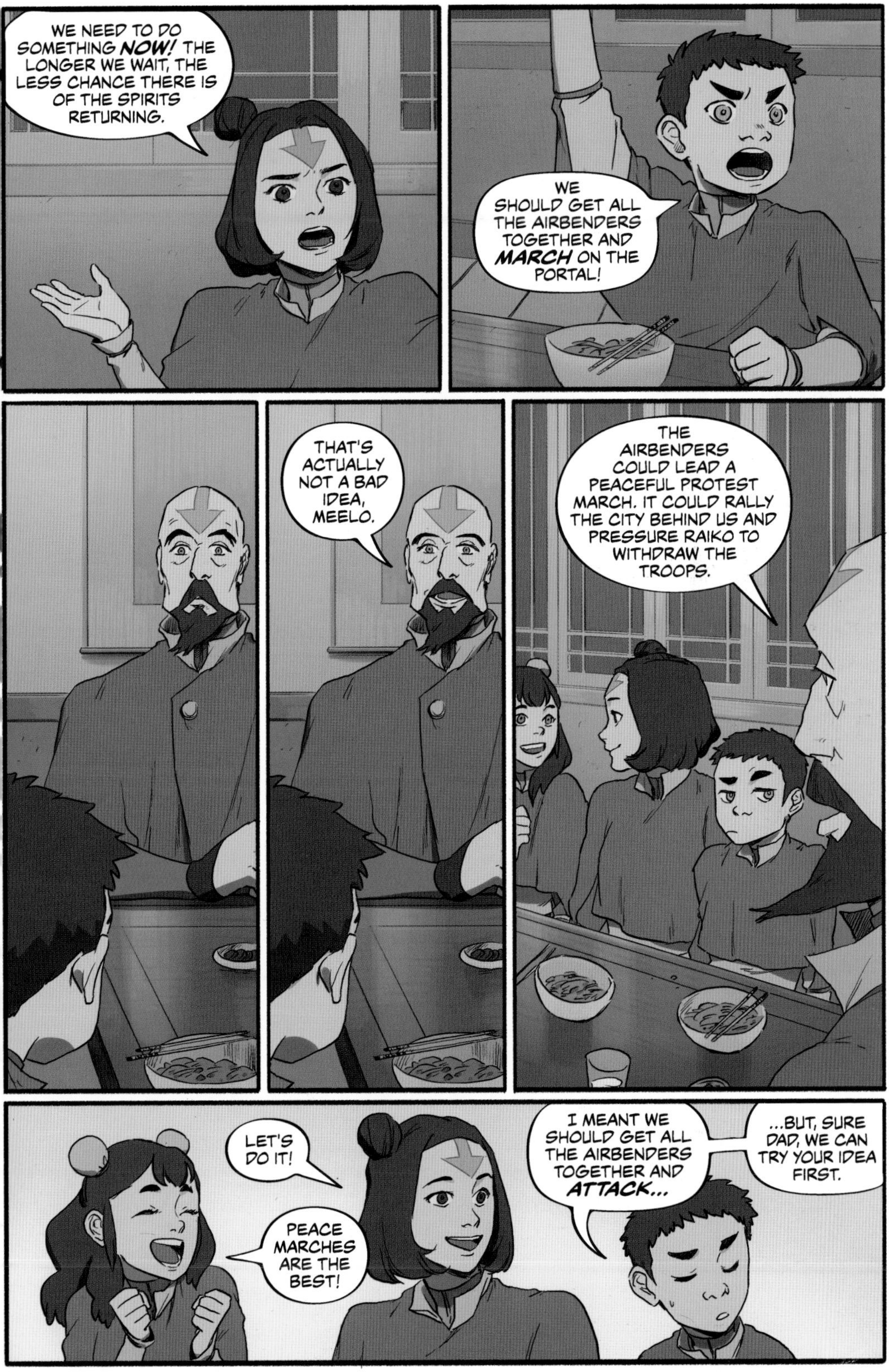
WE NEED TO DO SOMETHING NOW! THE LONGER WE WAIT, THE LESS CHANCE THERE IS OF THE SPIRITS RETURNING.
WE SHOULD GET ALL THE AIRBENDERS TOGETHER AND MARCH ON THE PORTAL!
THAT'S ACTUALLY NOT A BAD IDEA, MEELO.
THE AIRBENDERS COULD LEAD A PEACEFUL PROTEST MARCH. IT COULD RALLY THE CITY BEHIND US AND PRESSURE RAIKO TO WITHDRAW THE TROOPS.
LET'S DO IT!
PEACE MARCHES ARE THE BEST!
I MEANT WE SHOULD GET ALL THE AIRBENDERS TOGETHER AND ATTACK...
...BUT, SURE DAD, WE CAN TRY YOUR IDEA FIRST.

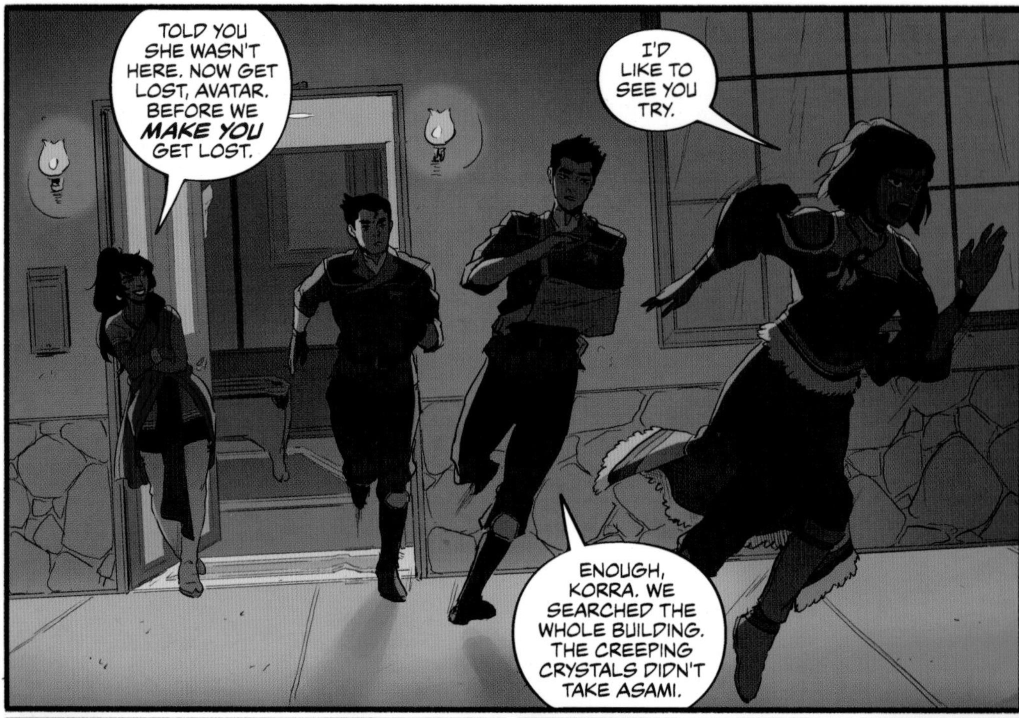
TOLD YOU SHE WASN'T HERE. NOW GET LOST, AVATAR. BEFORE WE *MAKE YOU* GET LOST.
I'D LIKE TO SEE YOU TRY.
ENOUGH, KORRA. WE SEARCHED THE WHOLE BUILDING. THE CREEPING CRYSTALS DIDN'T TAKE ASAMI.

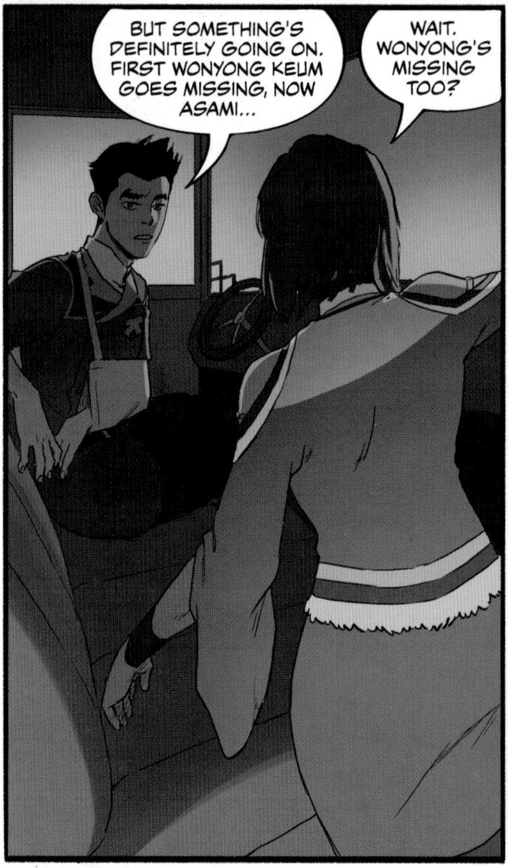
BUT SOMETHING'S DEFINITELY GOING ON. FIRST WONYONG KEUM GOES MISSING, NOW ASAMI...
WAIT. WONYONG'S MISSING TOO?

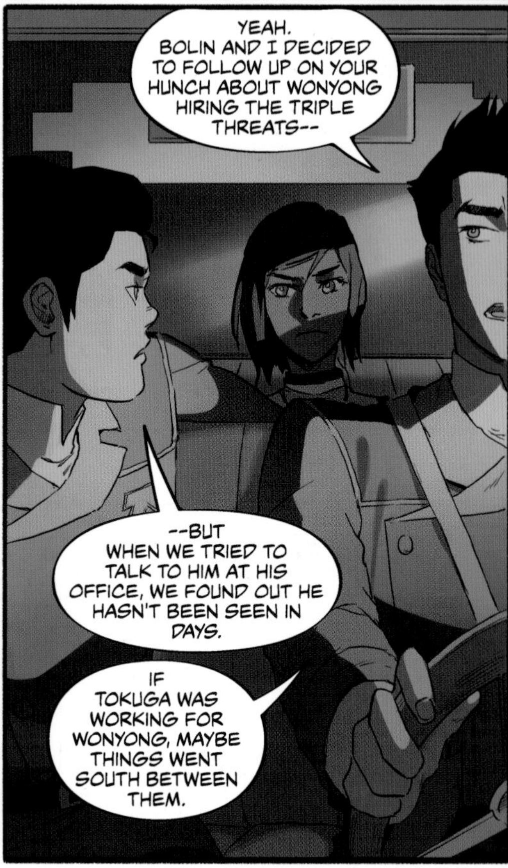
YEAH. BOLIN AND I DECIDED TO FOLLOW UP ON YOUR HUNCH ABOUT WONYONG HIRING THE TRIPLE THREATS--
--BUT WHEN WE TRIED TO TALK TO HIM AT HIS OFFICE, WE FOUND OUT HE HASN'T BEEN SEEN IN DAYS.
IF TOKUGA WAS WORKING FOR WONYONG, MAYBE THINGS WENT SOUTH BETWEEN THEM.

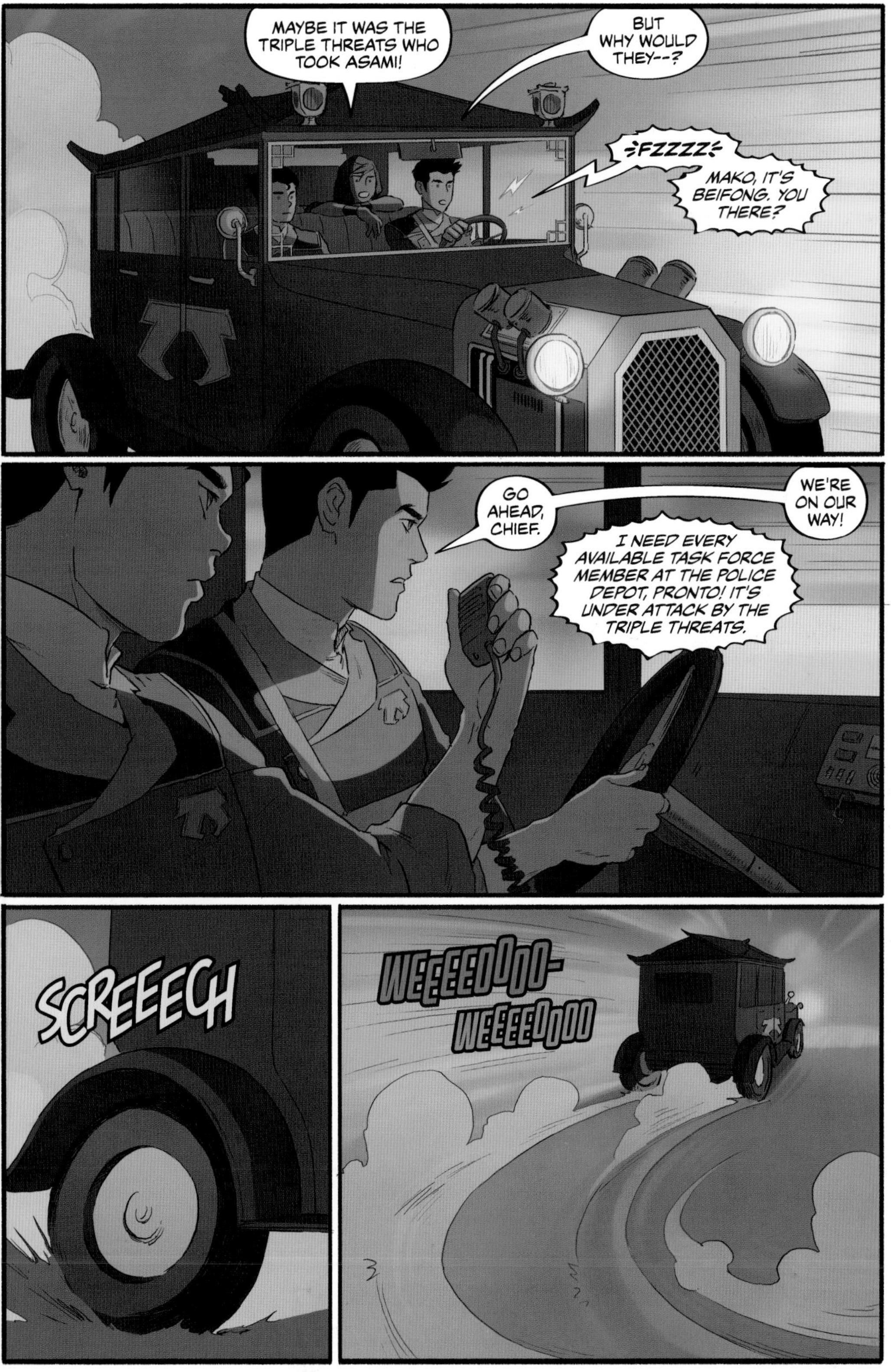
MAYBE IT WAS THE TRIPLE THREATS WHO TOOK ASAMI!
BUT WHY WOULD THEY--?
FZZZZ
MAKO, IT'S BEIFONG. YOU THERE?
GO AHEAD, CHIEF.
I NEED EVERY AVAILABLE TASK FORCE MEMBER AT THE POLICE DEPOT, PRONTO! IT'S UNDER ATTACK BY THE TRIPLE THREATS.
WE'RE ON OUR WAY!
SCREEECH
WEEEEOOOO-
WEEEEOOOO

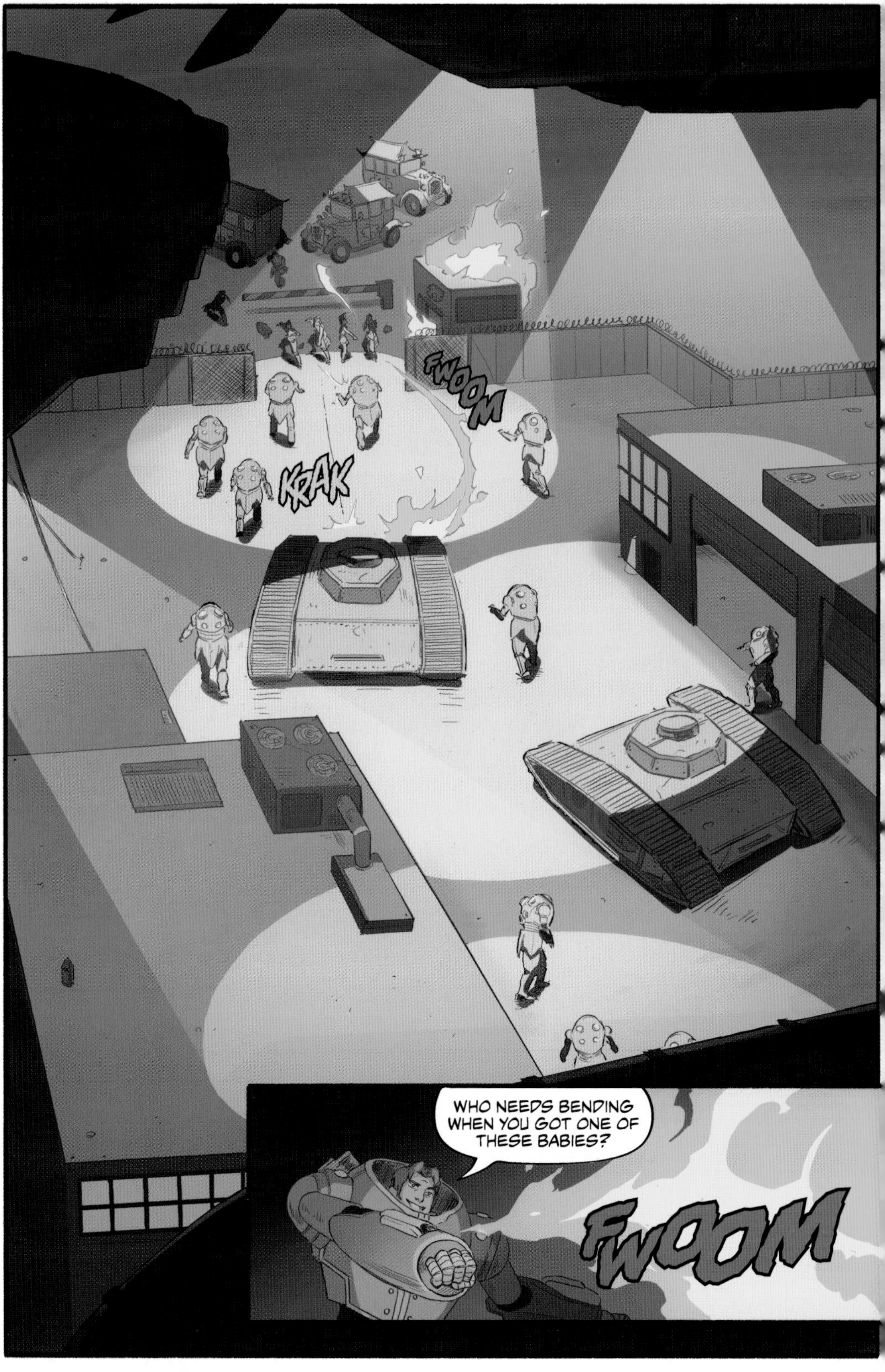
FWOOM
KRAK
WHO NEEDS BENDING WHEN YOU GOT ONE OF THESE BABIES?
FWOOM

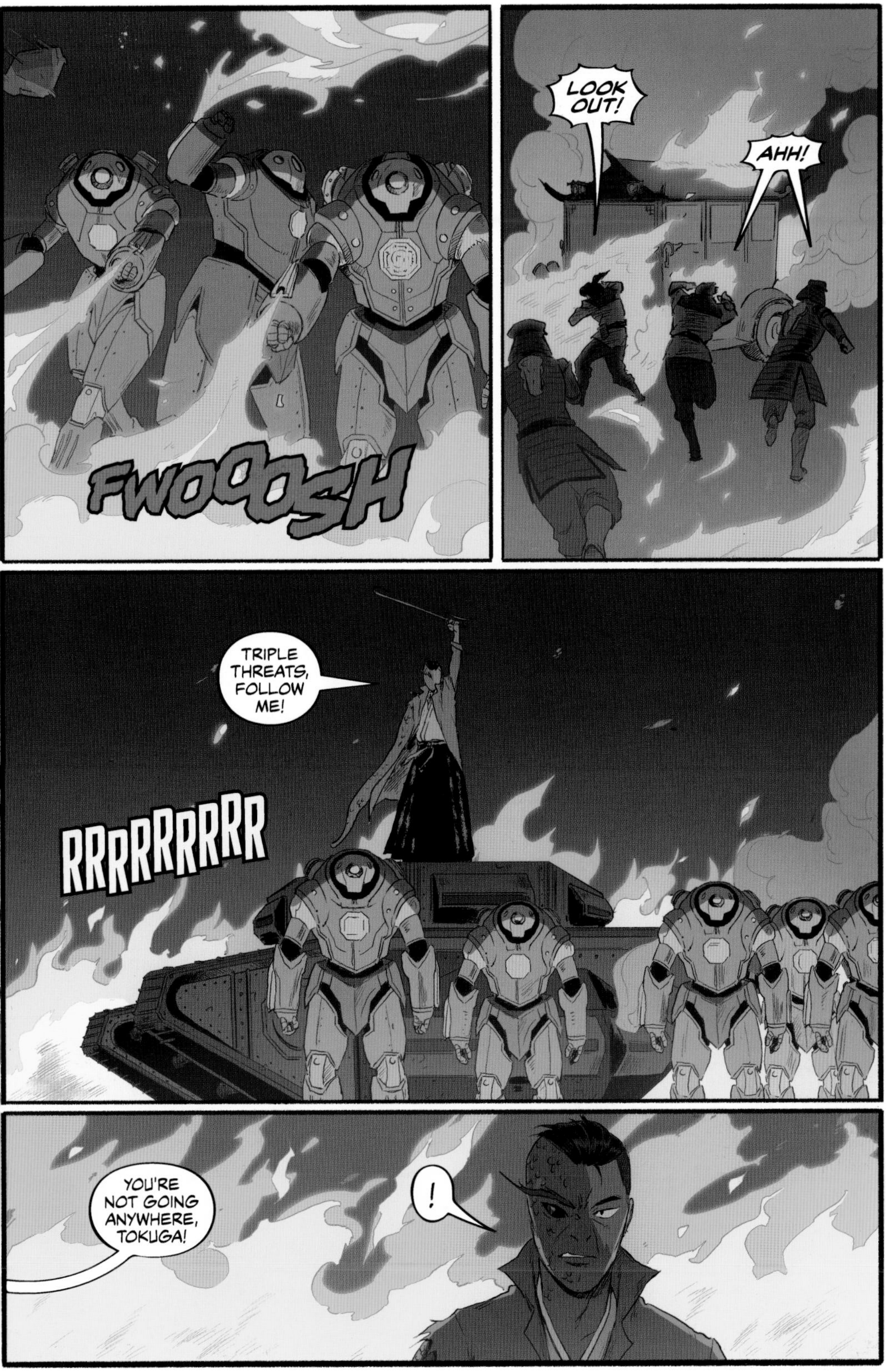
FWOOOSH
LOOK OUT!
AHH!
TRIPLE THREATS, FOLLOW ME!
RRRRRRRRR
YOU'RE NOT GOING ANYWHERE, TOKUGA!
!

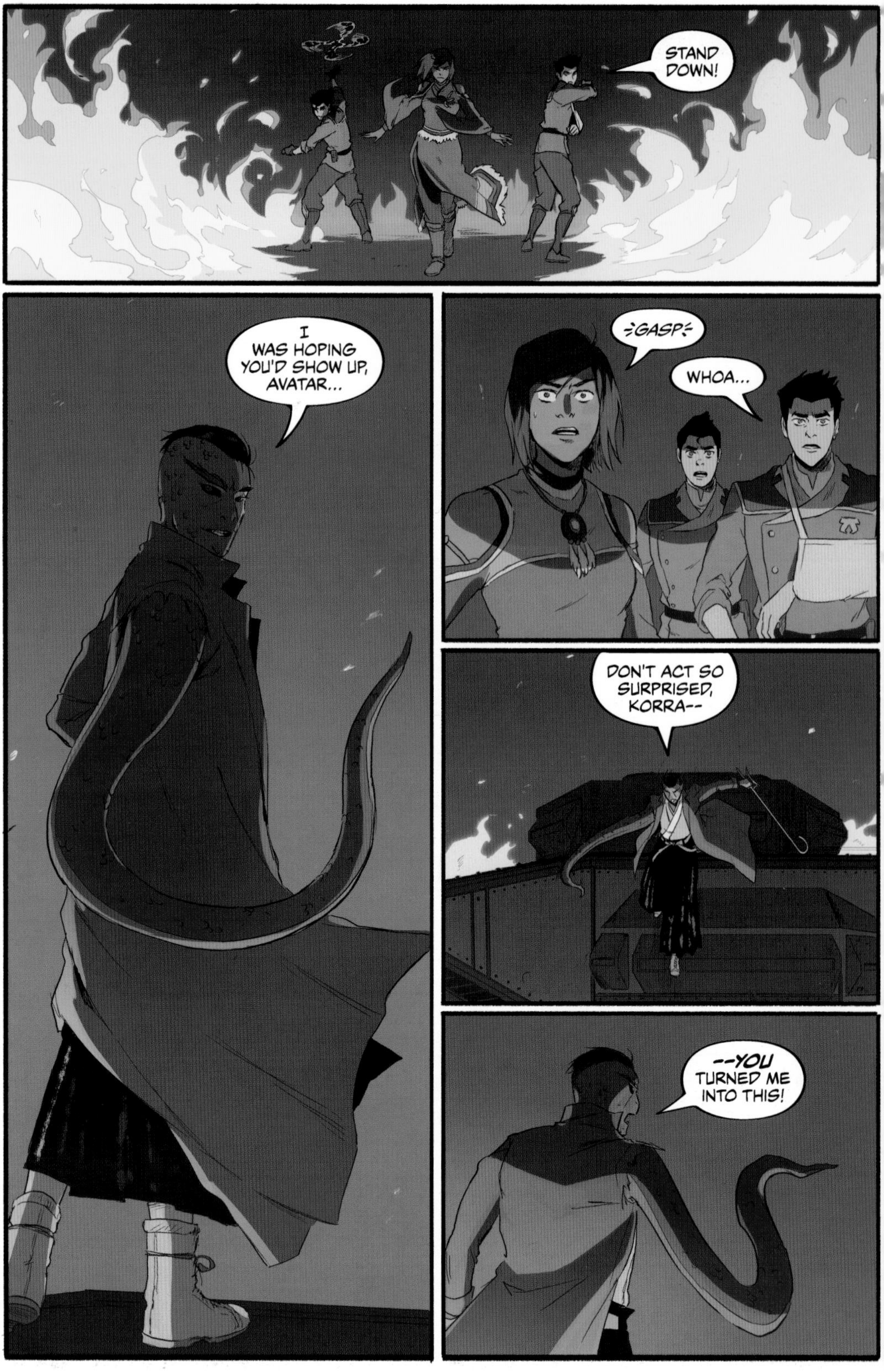
STAND DOWN!
I WAS HOPING YOU'D SHOW UP, AVATAR...
GASP
WHOA...
DON'T ACT SO SURPRISED, KORRA--
--YOU TURNED ME INTO THIS!

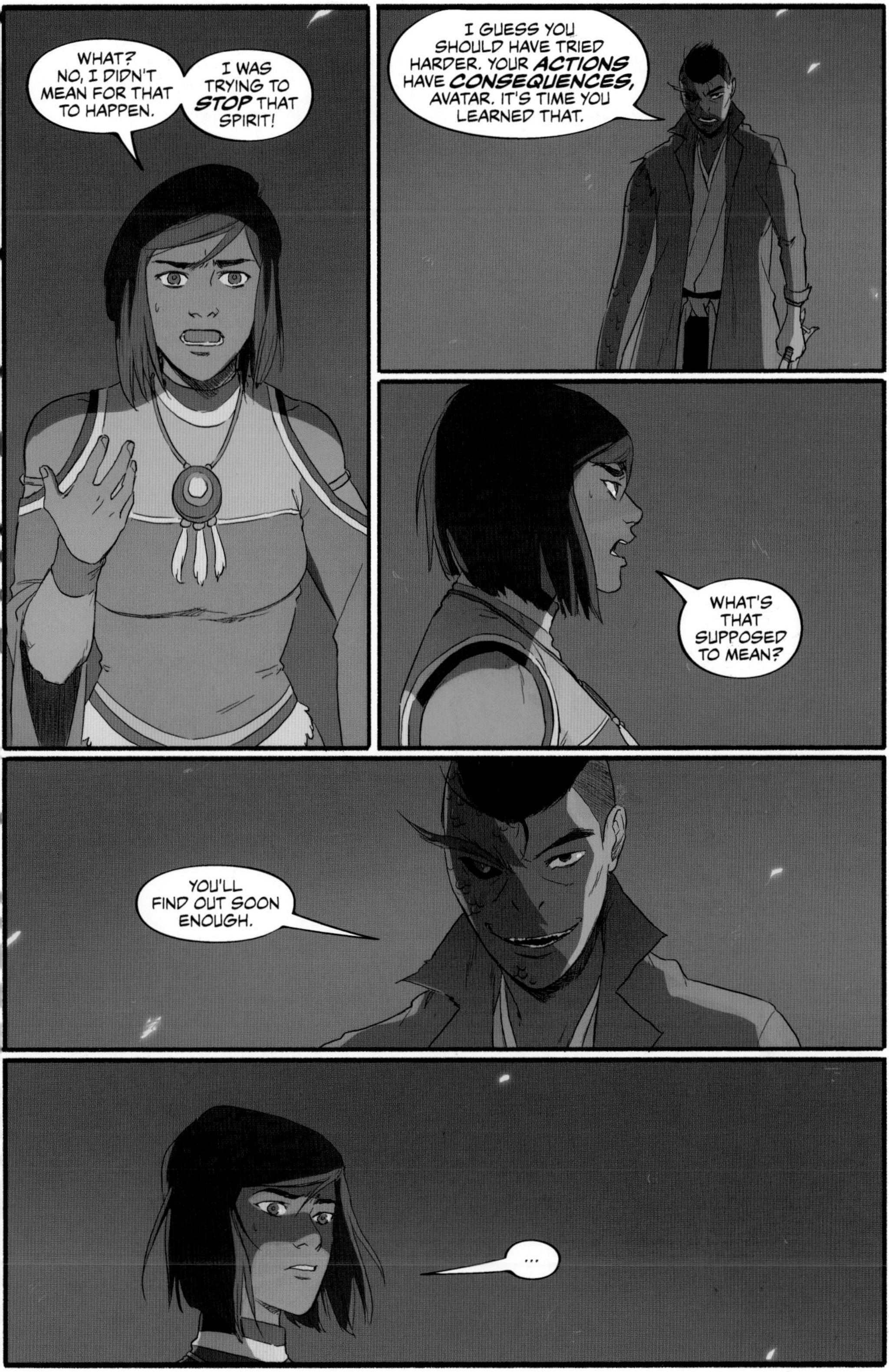
WHAT? NO, I DIDN'T MEAN FOR THAT TO HAPPEN.
I WAS TRYING TO STOP THAT SPIRIT!
I GUESS YOU SHOULD HAVE TRIED HARDER. YOUR ACTIONS HAVE CONSEQUENCES, AVATAR. IT'S TIME YOU LEARNED THAT.
WHAT'S THAT SUPPOSED TO MEAN?
YOU'LL FIND OUT SOON ENOUGH.
...

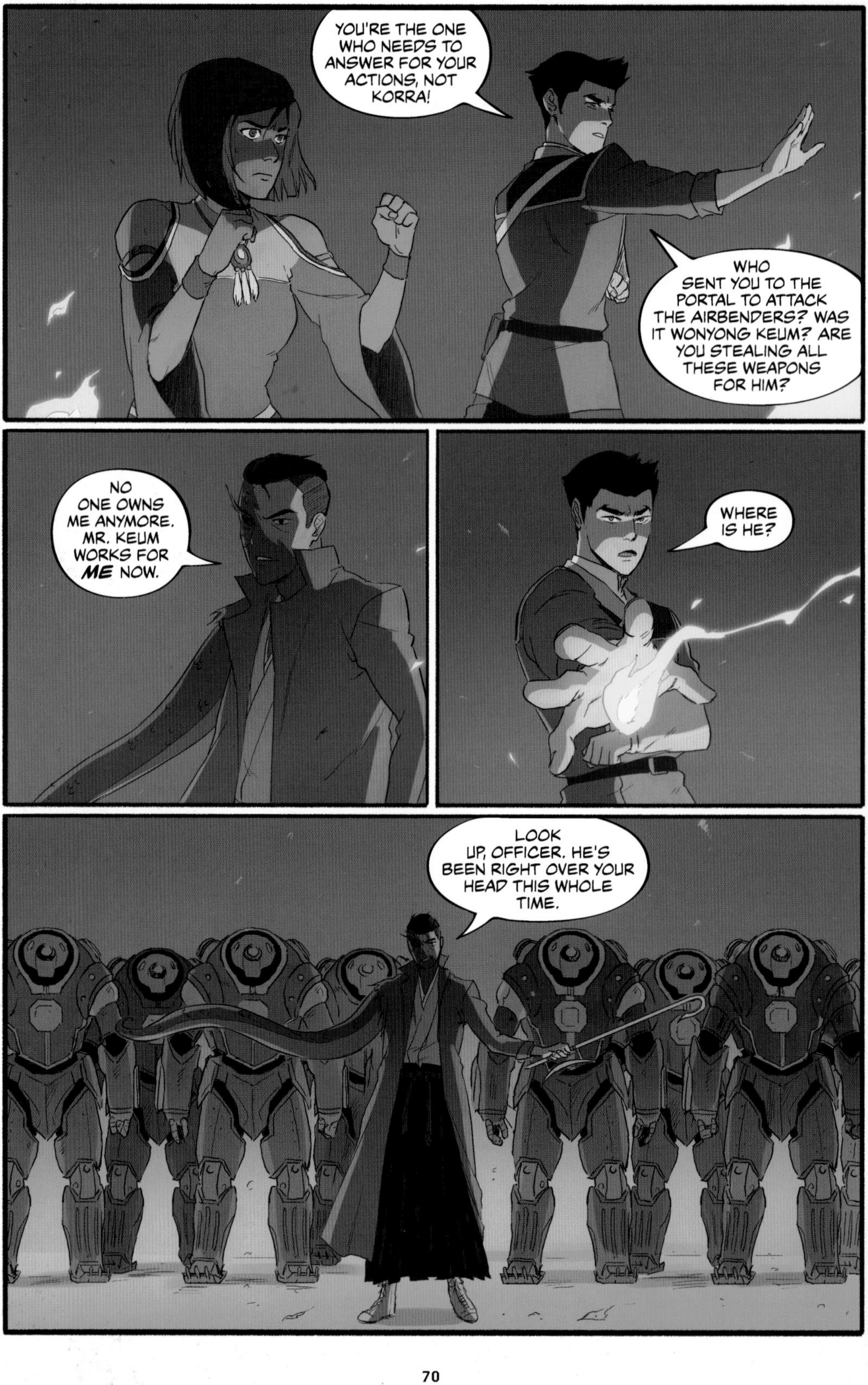
YOU'RE THE ONE WHO NEEDS TO ANSWER FOR YOUR ACTIONS, NOT KORRA!
WHO SENT YOU TO THE PORTAL TO ATTACK THE AIRBENDERS? WAS IT WONYONG KEUM? ARE YOU STEALING ALL THESE WEAPONS FOR HIM?
NO ONE OWNS ME ANYMORE. MR. KEUM WORKS FOR ***ME*** NOW.
WHERE IS HE?
LOOK UP, OFFICER. HE'S BEEN RIGHT OVER YOUR HEAD THIS WHOLE TIME.

IS THAT...?

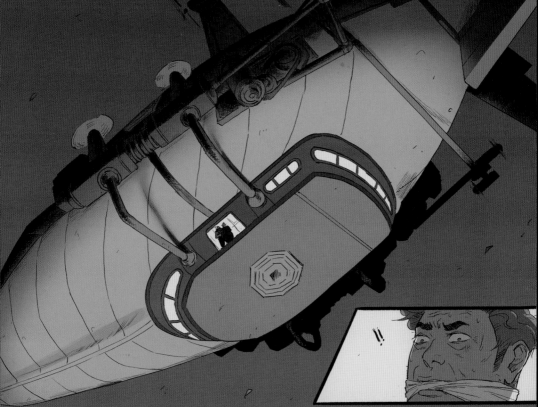

!!

MMMMPH!

RELEASE MR. KEUM IMMEDIATELY AND SURRENDER YOURSELVES!

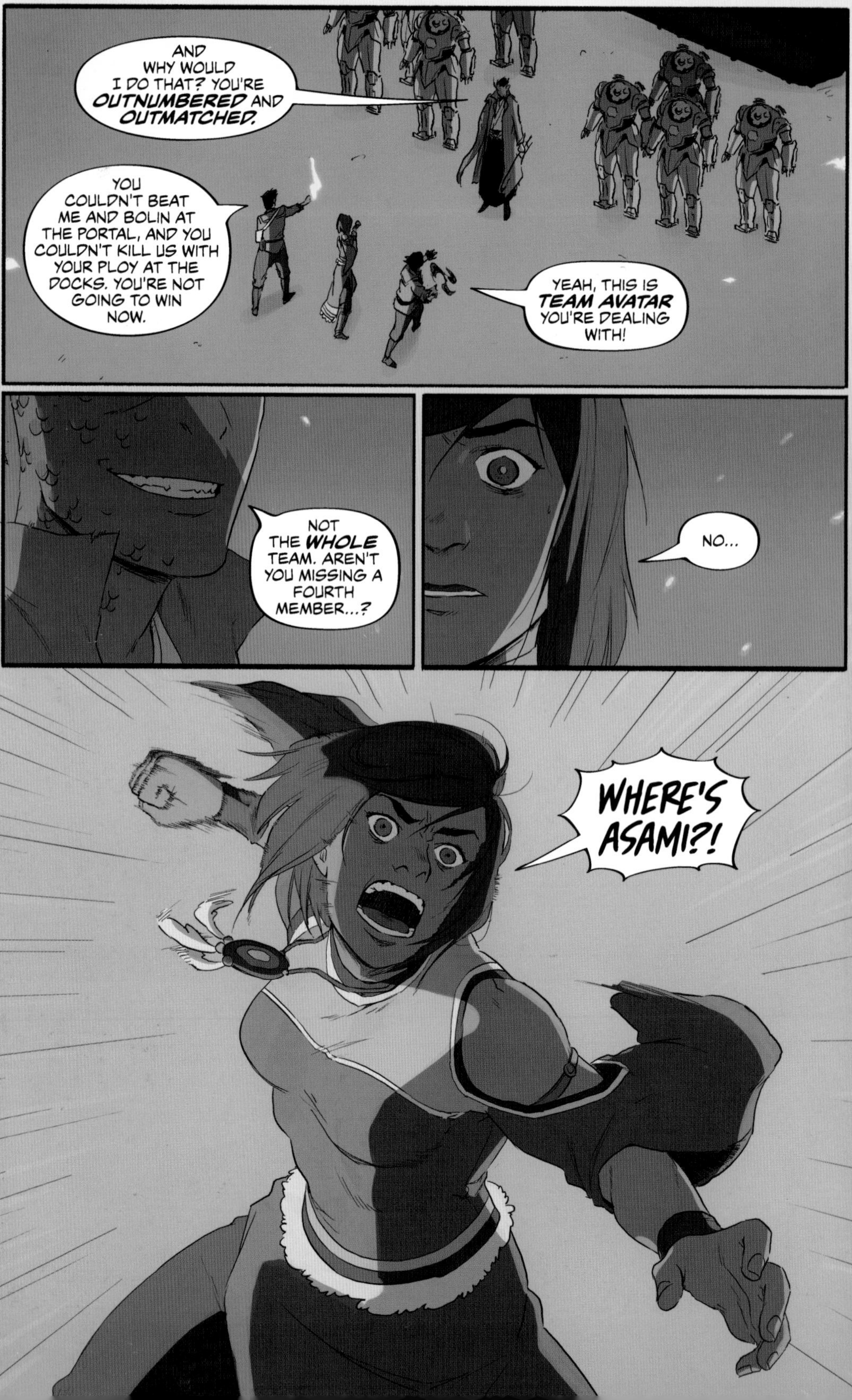
AND WHY WOULD I DO THAT? YOU'RE **OUTNUMBERED** AND **OUTMATCHED.**
YOU COULDN'T BEAT ME AND BOLIN AT THE PORTAL, AND YOU COULDN'T KILL US WITH YOUR PLOY AT THE DOCKS. YOU'RE NOT GOING TO WIN NOW.
YEAH, THIS IS **TEAM AVATAR** YOU'RE DEALING WITH!
NOT THE **WHOLE** TEAM. AREN'T YOU MISSING A FOURTH MEMBER...?
NO...
WHERE'S ASAMI?!

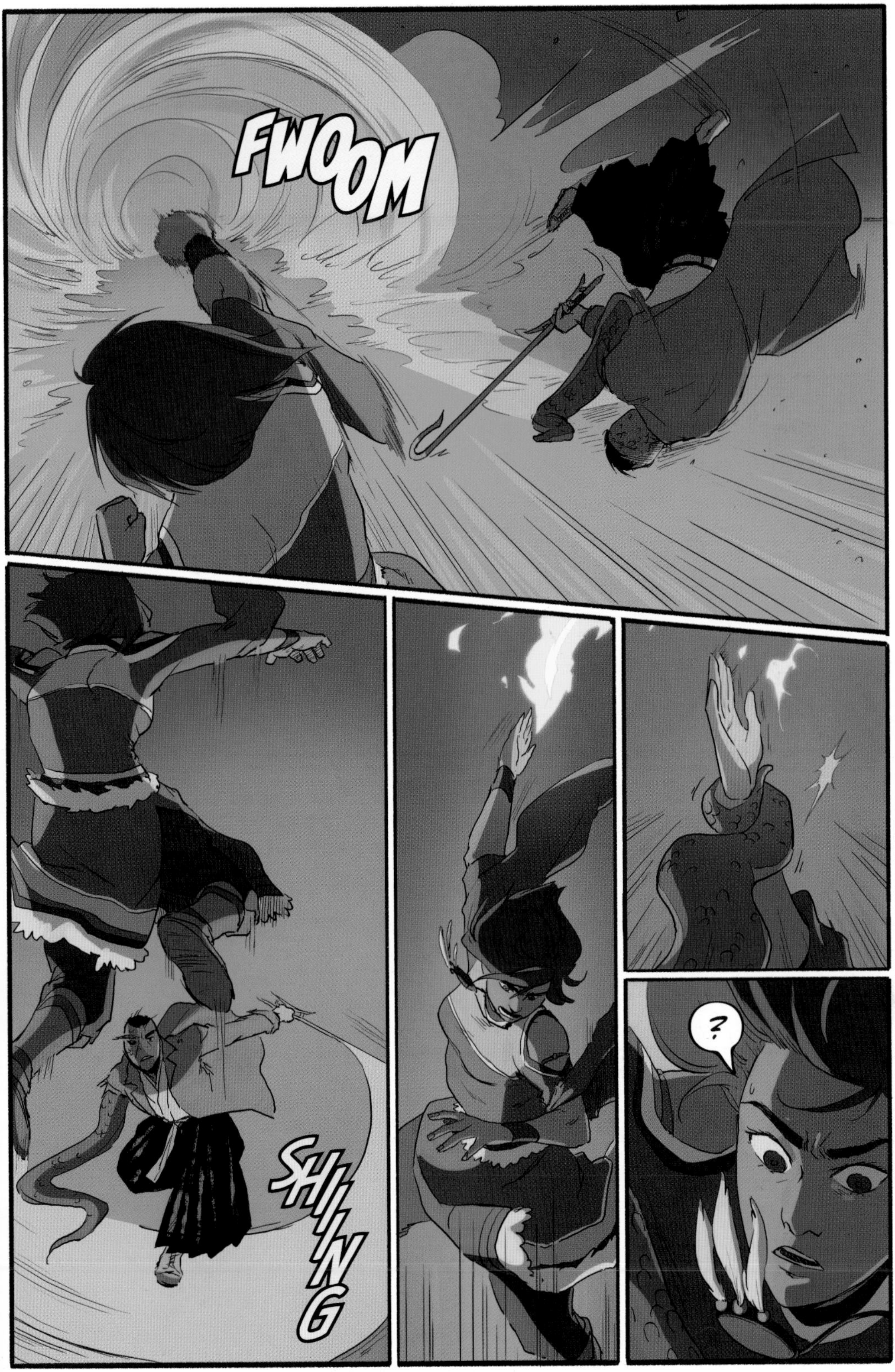
FWOOM
SHIING
?

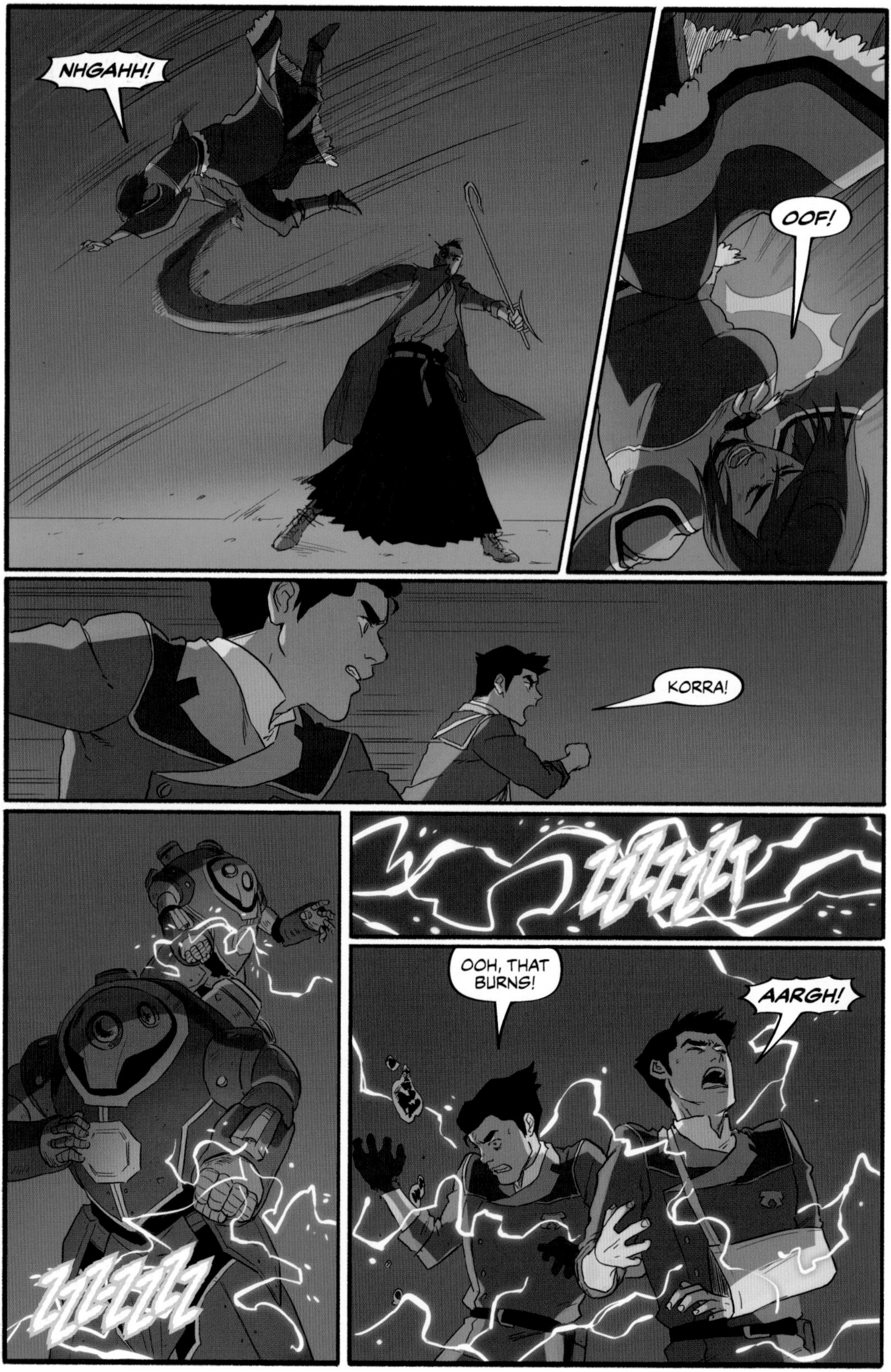
NHGAHH!
OOF!
KORRA!
ZZZZZZZ
ZZZZZZZ
OOH, THAT BURNS!
AARGH!

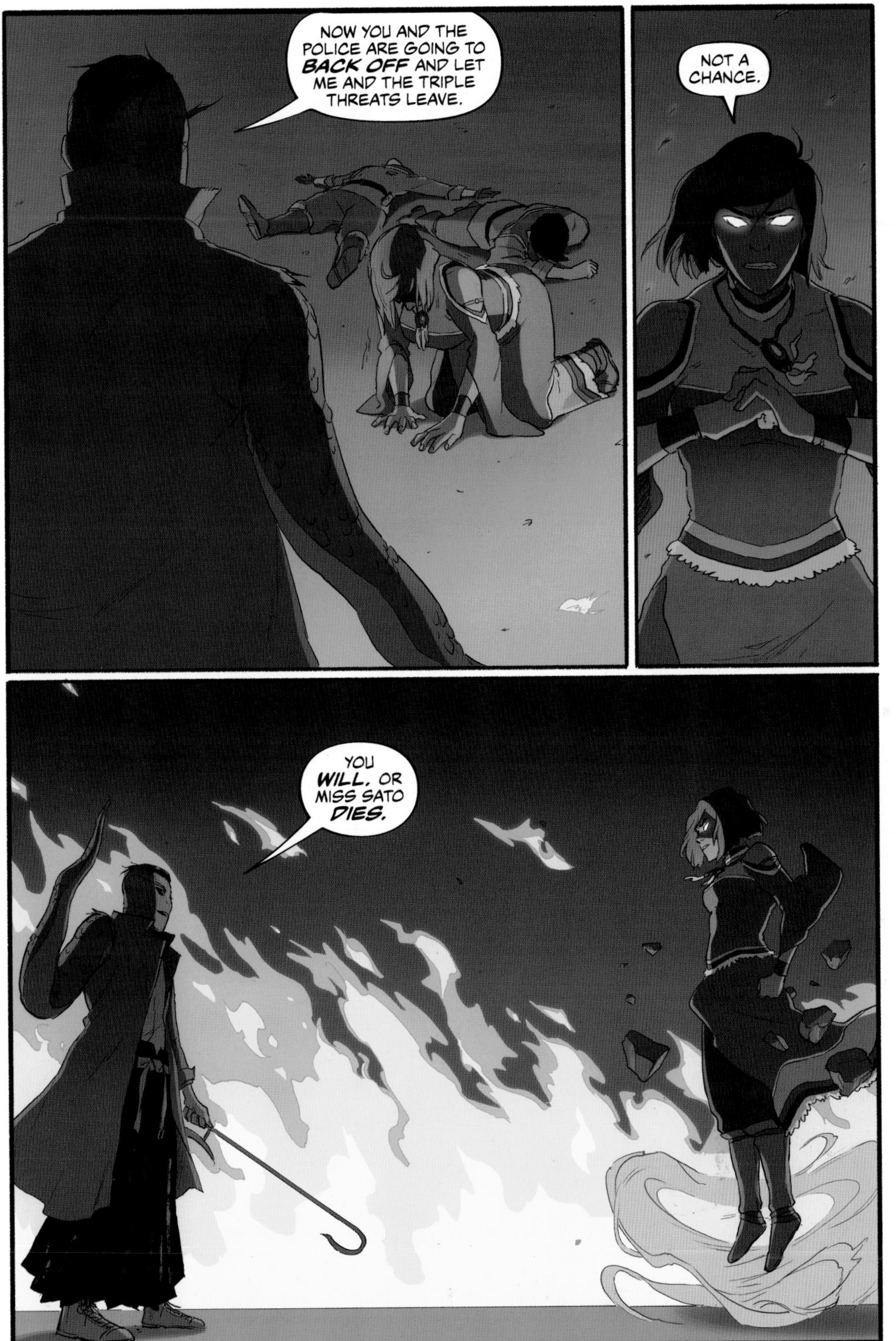
NOW YOU AND THE POLICE ARE GOING TO *BACK OFF* AND LET ME AND THE TRIPLE THREATS LEAVE.
NOT A CHANCE.
YOU *WILL*, OR MISS SATO *DIES*.

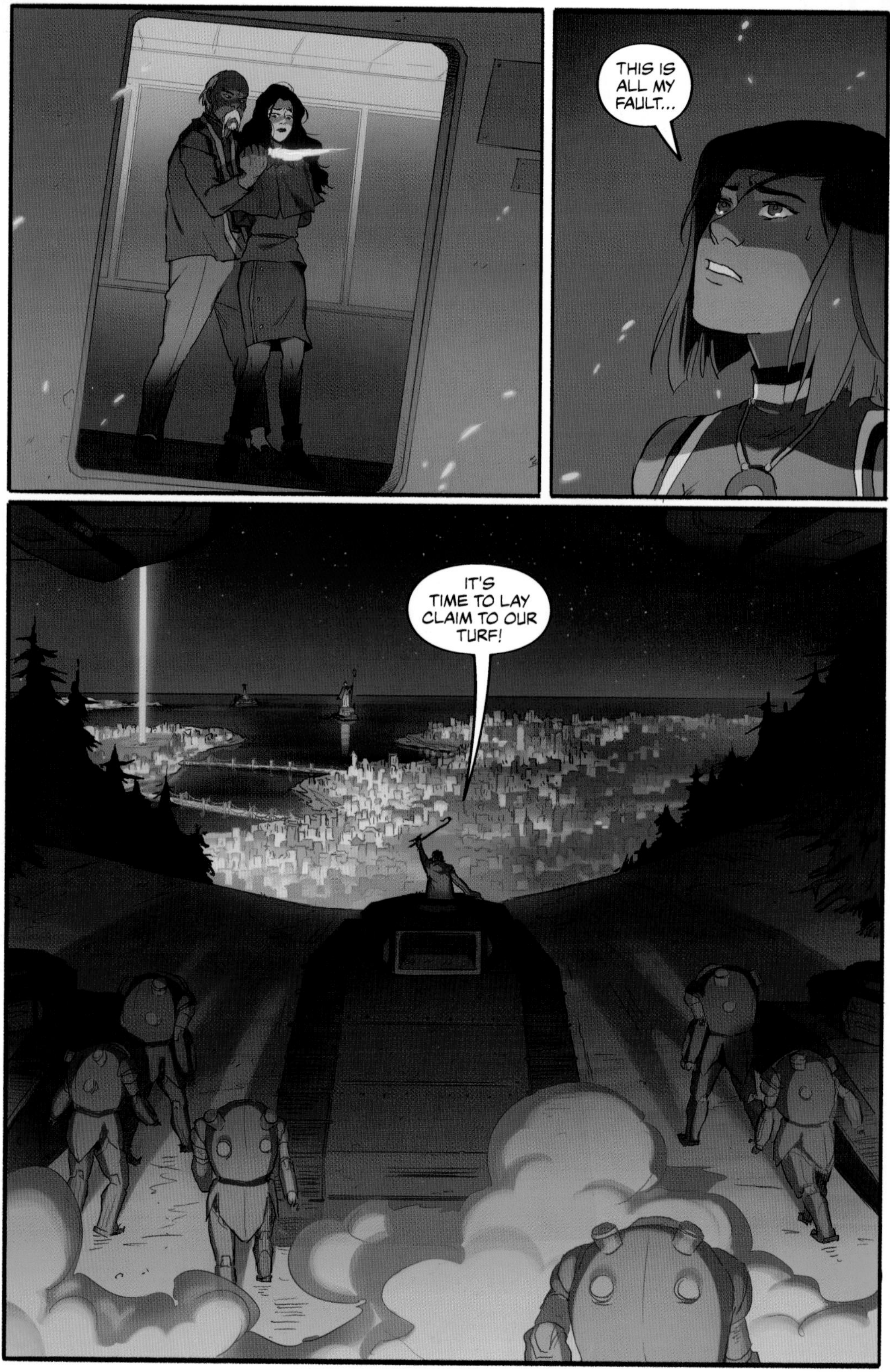
THIS IS ALL MY FAULT...
IT'S TIME TO LAY CLAIM TO OUR TURF!

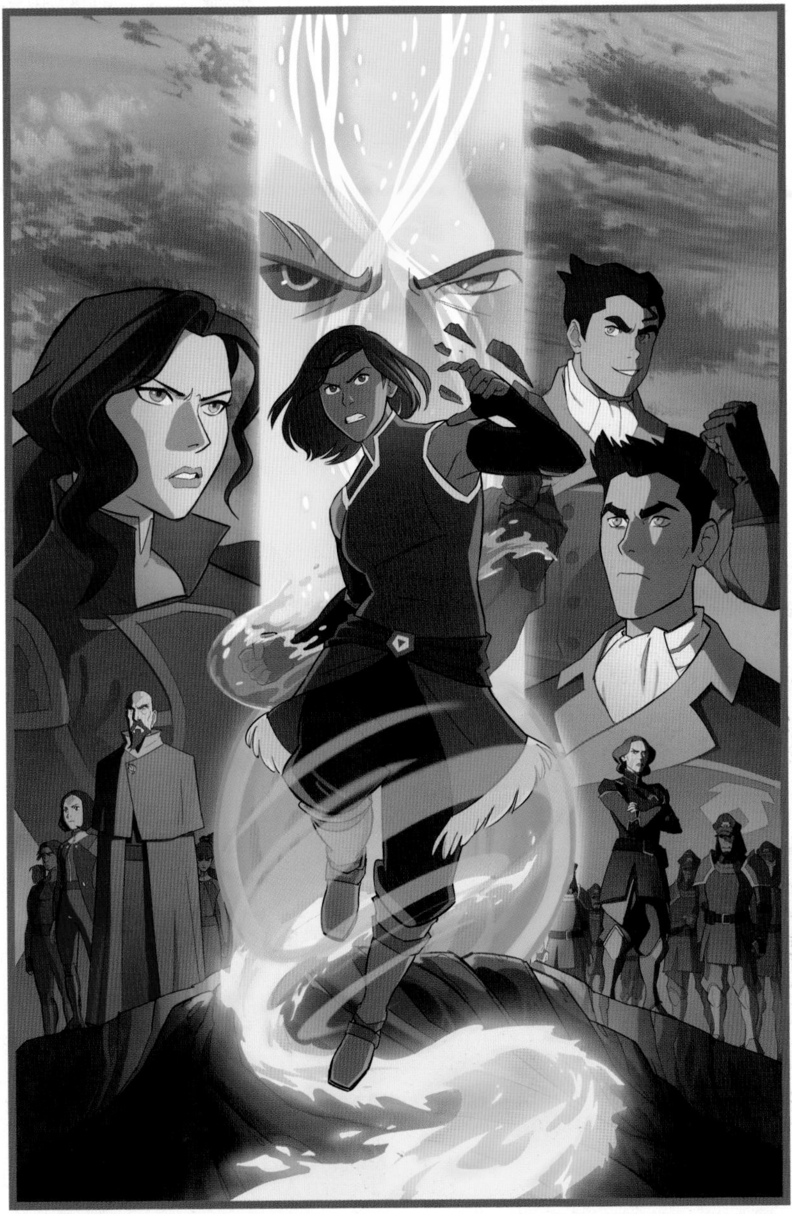

COMING IN JUNE 2018!

The final showdown at the spirit portal!

TURF WARS • PART THREE

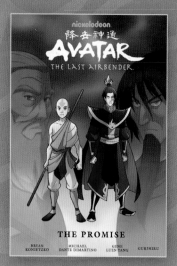

nickelodeon
AVATAR
THE LAST AIRBENDER
THE PROMISE
BRYAN KONIETZKO
MICHAEL DANTE DIMARTINO
GENE LUEN YANG
GURIHIRU

AVATAR
THE LAST AIRBENDER

Avatar: The Last Airbender—
The Promise Library Edition
978-1-61655-074-5 $39.99

Avatar: The Last Airbender—
The Promise Part 1
978-1-59582-811-8 $10.99

Avatar: The Last Airbender—
The Promise Part 2
978-1-59582-875-0 $10.99

Avatar: The Last Airbender—
The Promise Part 3
978-1-59582-941-2 $10.99

AVATAR

Avatar: The Last Airbender—
The Search Library Edition
978-1-61655-226-8 $39.99

Avatar: The Last Airbender—
The Search Part 1
978-1-61655-054-7 $10.99

Avatar: The Last Airbender—
The Search Part 2
978-1-61655-190-2 $10.99

Avatar: The Last Airbender—
The Search Part 3
978-1-61655-184-1 $10.99

AVATAR
THE LAST AIRBENDER
THE SEARCH
MICHAEL DANTE DiMARTINO

nickelodeon
AVATAR
THE LAST AIRBENDER
THE RIFT
BRYAN KONIETZKO
MICHAEL DANTE DIMARTINO
GENE LUEN YANG
GURIHIRU

AVATAR

Avatar: The Last Airbender—
The Rift Library Edition
978-1-61655-550-4 $39.99

Avatar: The Last Airbender—
The Rift Part 1
978-1-61655-295-4 $10.99

Avatar: The Last Airbender—
The Rift Part 2
978-1-61655-296-1 $10.99

Avatar: The Last Airbender—
The Rift Part 3
978-1-61655-297-8 $10.99